The Fragrance of Light

A Journey Into Buddhist Wisdom

THE FRAGRANCE OF LIGHT

A Journey Into Buddhist Wisdom

Compiled and Edited by

John Paraskevopoulos

SOPHIA PERENNIS

First published in the USA
by Sophia Perennis
an imprint of Angelico Press
© John Paraskevopoulos 2015

Series editor: James R. Wetmore

For information, address:
4709 Briar Knoll Dr.
Kettering, OH 45429
www.@angelicopress.com
info@angelicopress.com

ISBN 978-1-59731-145-8 (pbk: alk. paper)

Front Cover: Artwork by Gabriela Stauffer
Back Cover: 'Spring Landscape' (1672) by Kanyō Tanyū
[*Edo Period, ink on silk*]
(Freer Gallery of Art, Smithsonian Institution, Washington, DC:
Gift of Charles Lang Freer, F1892.28).
Cover Design: Laura Silvestri (AliaGrafica)

Sentient beings who are mindful of Amida Buddha are like persons who, imbued with incense, bear its fragrance on their bodies; hence, they are called 'those adorned with the fragrance of light.'

Śūraṅgama Samādhi Sūtra

CONTENTS

Acknowledgments x

Preface 1

CHAPTER ONE: Where We Find Ourselves
Impermanence, Suffering and the Human Condition 5

CHAPTER TWO: Ultimate Reality
Source and Destination 37

CHAPTER THREE: Living the Way
Signposts to Emancipation 59

CHAPTER FOUR: Immeasurable Life
Amida Buddha and the Pure Land 83

Appendix: *Voices of Light* 123
Biographical Index 147
Sources 156

ACKNOWLEDGMENTS

Sincere thanks are due to the Reverend George Gatenby, the Reverend Dr. Mark Healsmith, Mr. Alex Minchinton, Dr. Luc Schneider and Mr. Petros Theodorides for their invaluable suggestions, which have served to make this a better work than it might have otherwise been.

I would also like to extend my sincere gratitude to the International Association of Buddhist Culture for its generous grant in support of the preparation of this book.

Preface

The following work seeks to introduce readers to the rich vein of spiritual knowledge that is to be found in the countless scriptures and texts that make up the Buddhist tradition. While many such anthologies already exist, this one has a particular aim in mind. Firstly, it seeks to address both our intellectual and affective needs with a focus on passages that have a poetic or evocative quality—that is, beauty in both content and form. This is especially important in this day and age when there is a paucity of inspiring works in contemporary Buddhism. These teachings, over two thousand years, have developed into a magnificent repository of wisdom as witnessed by its many faithful who have actually experienced that of which they speak—it is a major testament to a living path that has engaged the hearts and minds of millions, something which it has continued to do up to the present time.

In considering a spiritual tradition, it is difficult to speak with any authority if one is relying solely on an academic study of texts or on the linguistic analysis of technical terms. As useful as these can be, they cannot convey the full flavour of what such works are telling us unless one has awakened—in some measure—to the same truth that impelled its authors to commit them to writing in the first place. Moreover, this work also aims to foster a renewed interest in the spiritual, metaphysical and cosmic aspects of Buddhist thought which are often neglected or obscured in current treatments of the subject but which, doubtlessly, lend the teachings a richer and deeper dimension.

The anthology quite consciously represents a perspective that accepts the veracity of higher realities, does not consider a materialist or scientific view of life as either an exhaustive or definitive account of our existence and which recognises the deep spiritual yearnings of humanity as pointing to something very real and of the utmost importance to our lives. The task of this book, therefore, is to help initiate the process towards a more positive reflection on, and engagement with, the Buddhist faith across its entire spectrum. In our current climate of spiritual malaise and confusion, surely no task could be more urgent.

The passages selected are from both ancient and modern authors, many of whom are not well known but who deserve wider recognition. They cover all the great themes of the Dharma such as human suffering, ultimate reality, our moral lives, practice and devotion. In addition to Buddhist sources, we have also included a very small handful of passages reflecting Taoist thought (especially given the influence of this tradition on Buddhism in the Far East) as well as from poets over the ages whose perspectives have been inspired by these spiritualities. We believe that these inclusions add to the interest and appeal of the collection.

It is only proper that the author declare his hand at this point and make known his personal association with the Pure Land tradition, a fact which is reflected in the compilation of this anthology. Apart from believing that this highly influential school has much to offer modern seekers, it is also significant that it is the most popular form of Buddhism in East Asia. In its more developed form as Shin Buddhism, it also represents, in many ways, its logical terminus.

Some of the themes that are explored in these chapters may seem repetitive in parts. This is because the aim is essentially *mnemonic*— something to assist the memory in assimilating the truths contained therein with a view to provoking, and subsequently reinforcing, the insights to which they may give rise. This technique was commonly used in the early days of Buddhism when it was largely an oral tradition and where 'hearing' the Dharma over and over again led to its gradual permeation into the hearts and minds of listeners who were thereby able to internalise its truths.

The purpose of this anthology is none other than to present this tradition at its finest; to showcase its many hidden jewels in the hope that they will transform the reader and lead them to aspire to seek the way of the Buddha through a wisdom that is powerful, sobering and joyous.

J.P.
Canberra
Festival of Vesak
May 2015

CHAPTER ONE

WHERE WE FIND OURSELVES

—Impermanence, Suffering and the Human Condition

Introduction

The collection of passages in this chapter present a sustained and unflinching assessment of the human condition in a way that is sure to give us cause for serious reflection. No one will be able to deny the truth of what is stated here or the depth of insight that has been brought to bear in examining the reality of our lives.

A common charge levied against the Buddhist teachings is that they are 'pessimistic', insofar as they often depict our life in this world as unsatisfactory and full of suffering. However, the Buddha offered clear reasons for why this is so and gave advice on what might be done about it. In fact, it would be truer to say that Buddhism is neither pessimistic nor optimistic. Both perspectives represent one-sided distortions that do not reflect the way things are. Pessimism usually conveys an outlook of relentless negativity, or even despair, that sees no hope in the prospect of any positive change in our lives or in the condition of society. It would appear that this is a widely-held view among many people in the world and for reasons that are not hard to find. Nevertheless, despite ostensible similarities between such an outlook and the teachings we find in the Buddhist tradition, there are important differences and they have to do with the solution proposed for our troubled earthly lives. On the other hand, optimism is the tendency to see everything in a favourable light despite the most severe contradictions presented by the realities of everyday life. While an optimistic view is often praised as healthy and sanguine, more often than not it fails to do justice to the harsh truths of our existential condition, which no amount of 'positive thinking' can dispel. In this way, it is in constant danger of lacking credibility.

One does not get closer to the truth by sweeping distressing or unpleasant matters under the carpet and insisting that they do not exist or are not as bad as they seem. Such an attitude seeks a resolution to the problem at the wrong level. In his attempt to understand life in our world, the Buddha was driven by the quest for truth, however painful or unpalatable it might be. In deeply contemplating the way things are, he sought to be realistic in his assessment; neither hopelessly negative nor naively optimistic. He also observed that we tend to avoid difficult truths about life when they challenge our pre-conceptions, interests and attachments. We feel intensely vulnerable when circumstances run counter to our aspirations, because we fear that they may be undermined altogether.

The Buddha clearly recognised this and felt immense compassion and concern for ordinary people who suffered in this way. He saw such affliction as both a form of blindness (or lack of wisdom) and as a raging fire in which our deep-seated desires threaten to consume us. The passages in this chapter depict, often in very vivid and even moving language, how we are all held captive to our insatiable appetite for love, wealth, fame, power and even for life itself. But what do such desires represent? Seeing as they are often unfulfilled or disappointing when they are met, how do we account for their overwhelming force in our lives? And what makes us feel so troubled by the imperma-nence of things?

Perhaps it is not the fact of our desire, as such, that is the problem but the objects to which it is directed. Of course, many desires are natural and proper but also often elusive in their fulfillment. Yet they remain quite powerful regardless of where they are focused. Nevertheless, to see the passages in this chapter as just an assault on everything we value and hold dear would be a mistake, not to mention a dishearten-ing exercise that may lead one to acute despondency. While acknowl-edging the truth of what these wise people are saying, one can also take their insights as pointing to something beyond the mere descrip-tion of suffering and unhappiness.

The constant reinforcement of this message on every page might serve to trigger an awakening, not only to the truth of life in all its sadness and disappointments but to the prospect of overcoming our fraught situation, from the vantage point of a more profound and lib-erating perspective that lies beyond this world of 'birth-and-death' (which Buddhists call *saṃsāra*). If not for this, how do we explain both our deepest longing for happiness and the lamentable fact that it is so difficult to secure in this world? Our very nature is telling us something about what we really are at our core and, in this, lies a vital clue to our enduring well-being.

In light of the above, the strong sentiments expressed in these passages are not just poetic expressions of disenchantment with the world but an accurate account of how things really are. This it does with the deeper aim of provoking an aspiration for that which transcends our realm of impermanence—an ineffable reality that is reflected in its fragmented traces; namely our precarious, but precious, earthly joys and the fragile beauty all around us. As one master in this collection reminds us, suffering can be a great teacher if only to instruct us in lessening our attachments to illusory sources of satisfaction and to seek true liberation in the Buddha's realm of light.

The Fragrance of Light

The greatest of human events are life and death.

CHANG PO-TUAN

This world is like a dream and all phenomena like echoes.

Avataṃsaka Sūtra

Our fragile body is easily dispersed, like ... flower petals in the spring. When the time comes, our temporal life passes away like leaves carried off by the winds of autumn.

KŪKAI

I watch people in the world
Throw away their lives lusting after things,
Never able to satisfy their desires,
Falling into deeper despair
And torturing themselves.
Even if they get what they want,
How long will they be able to enjoy it?
For one heavenly pleasure
They suffer ten torments of hell,
Binding themselves more firmly to the grindstone.
Such people are like monkeys
Frantically grasping for the moon in the water
And then falling into a whirlpool.
How endlessly those caught up in this floating world suffer.
Despite myself, I fret over them all night
And cannot stem my flow of tears.*

RYŌKAN

My foes will become nothing.
My friends will become nothing.
I too will become nothing.
Likewise all will become nothing.

---

* "The Buddhist point of view will appeal only to those people who are completely disillusioned with the world as it is, and with themselves; who are extremely sensitive to pain, suffering and any kind of turmoil; who have an extreme desire for happiness and a considerable capacity for renunciation. No Buddhist would assume that all men are either able or willing to understand this doctrine." (Edward Conze)

WHERE WE FIND OURSELVES

Just like a dream experience,
Whatever things I enjoy
Will become a memory.
Whatever has passed will not be seen again.

SHANTIDEVA

Yellow leaves hang on your tree of life. The messengers of death are waiting. You are going to travel far away. Have you any provision for the journey?

The Dhammapada

Someone who fails, even for a short while, to keep in mind the preciousness of time is no different from a corpse.

KENKŌ

The terrors of the calamities in the woeful states of misery
Are harsh and violent, continuous and manifold.

Avataṃsaka Sūtra

Sentient beings are spell-bound by folly and infatuation. They are needlessly haunted by the fear of death and old age, and do not seek the path of emancipation. Mortified with grief, anxiety and tribulation, they do not refrain from committing foul deeds. Clinging to their loved ones, they are always afraid of separation.... Trying to shun enmity, hatred and pain, they cherish more hatred.

VASUBANDHU

All phenomena, existing and apparent,
Are ever transient, changing and unstable;
But more especially the worldly life
Has no reality, no permanent gain [in it].
And so, instead of doing work that is profitless,
The Truth Divine I seek.

MILAREPA

It is enough, it would seem, to have been born into this world for us to desire many things.

KENKŌ

I'm so aware
That it's all unreal.
One by one, the things of this world pass on.
But why do I still grieve?

RYŌKAN

Our desires are countless, and anger, wrath, jealousy and envy are overwhelming, arising without pause; to the very last moment of life they do not cease, or disappear, or exhaust themselves.

SHINRAN

Consider this body! A painted puppet with jointed limbs; often suffering . . . full of imaginings, never permanent, forever changing . . . A house of bones is this body, bones covered with flesh and blood. Pride and hypocrisy dwell in this house as do old age and death.

The Dhammapada

Sentient beings whirl in a sea of craving and greed,
Shrouded by the web of ignorance, terribly oppressed;
Sentient beings, confused, have lost the right path;
Always going the wrong way, they enter a house of darkness.

Avataṃsaka Sūtra

If someone came and informed you that you would certainly lose your life the following day, what would you have to look forward to, what would you do to occupy yourself while waiting for this day to end? In what does the day we are now living differ from our last day? Much of our time during any day is wasted in eating and drinking, at stool, in sleeping, talking and walking. To engage in useless activities, to talk about useless things, and to think about useless matters during the brief moments of free time left to us is not only to waste this time, but to blot out days that extend into months and eventually into a whole lifetime. This is most foolish of all.

KENKŌ

Business men boast of their skill and cunning
But in wisdom they are like little children.
Bragging to each other of successful depredations,
They neglect to consider the ultimate fate of the body.

CH'EN TZU-ANG

WHERE WE FIND OURSELVES

The past is already past,
The future is not yet here,
The present never abides.
Things are constantly changing, with nothing on which to depend.
So many names and words confusingly self-created—
What is the use of wasting your life thus idly all day?

RYŌKAN

The sun at noon is exactly beginning to go down. And, when born, a creature is exactly beginning to die.

HUI-SHIH

The strong subdue the weak. They inflict serious injuries and kill each other; all devour their prey. Not knowing how to do good, they commit outrageous and unruly deeds. . . . The suffering of transmigration through dark and dismal realms is comparable to the severest and most painful punishment ever enforced by law. . . . Longing for death, they cannot die; craving for life, they cannot live. . . . In this world, you should extensively plant roots of virtue, be benevolent, give generously, abstain from breaking the precepts, be patient and diligent, teach people with sincerity and wisdom, do virtuous deeds and practice good. . . . But in this world much evil is committed and few are provided for naturally; people must work hard to get what they want. Since they intend to deceive each other, their minds are troubled and their bodies exhausted. . . . In this way, they are preoccupied with toil and have no time for rest.

Sūtra on the Buddha of Immeasurable Life

Some, surrounded by wife and children, friends and family, cannot cut the ties of affection that bind them. Others, seeing only their enemies and those they despise, never cease to rankle with loathing and vexation. Whatever people may do, they are just serving their own interests with all their energy, amassing the karma* that will carry them to . . . renewed existence.

HŌNEN

---

* "The doctrine of *karma* had its origins in India long before Buddhism appeared but has undergone great change under the influence of Buddhist thought. What a Buddhist means by karma is the acts and results of acts which are produced by our

Life seems easy for those who are, shamelessly, bold and self-assertive, crafty and cunning, sensuously selfish, wanton and impure, arrogant and insulting, rotting with corruption.

The Dhammapada

Alas, alas, you unfortunate beings,
Who cling to worldly things,
The deeper the grief, the longer that I think of you;
The deeper is my sorrow the longer that I taste of yours.
We whirl and whirl, till into Hell we fall;
For those whose karma brings sorrow's heart-ache,
Devotion of their life to Truth is, of all things, best.

MILAREPA

Of those I used to know, hardly one or two out of twenty or thirty remain. One dies in the morning, another is born in the evening— they come and go like froth on the water.

KAMO NO CHŌMEI

Earnestly resolve in your heart: this life is one night's lodging; this world but dream and illusion, so let it be as it may. As a means to taking your existence lightly and aspiring for the world beyond, you should become keenly aware that being alive is a matter of this day only, of the present moment alone. Realise this, and what is now scarcely endurable will be easily borne, and your endeavour for the world beyond will be dauntless. If you imagine even casually that your life will be long, things of this world will swell in importance and all those concerns unrelated to the aspiration for enlightenment will

free will. Acts in former states of existence have a profound influence upon our present condition. And it is often supposed that this involves a sort of fatalistic enslavement of our wills, destroying their freedom. But, on the contrary, our wills are fundamentally free to make moral choices and we are individually responsible for all our actions. Karma does, indeed, produce our dispositions and environment but not their activities which are still free. If we were to go on living [solely] from the stimulus which comes from the natural world, human society and purposed education, we would indeed be the slaves of our inherited karma; but the fact is that we are continually influenced within and without, and so are capable of volitions which produce new karma." (Harper Havelock Coates & Ryugaku Ishizuka, *Honen the Buddhist Saint: His Life and Teachings*, p. ix)

arise. . . . Ultimately, the key to liberation lies in setting your mind on impermanence.

KYŌBUTSU

All living beings, without exception, are subject to the universal law of change and decay. All people fall victim to disease, old age and death. When these calamities befall any person, nobody else can help. When a boy dies, his mother cannot take his place. When a mother becomes old and dies, her son cannot take her place. . . . According to the teaching of the Buddha, the destiny of all beings is determined by their individual karma, which means thoughts, words and deeds. As energy is imperishable, so is the influence of all action imperishable.

RYUCHI FUJII

The things encountered in samsaric existence prove the latent presence of enlightenment even while appearing to hide it.

MARCO PALLIS

When I think about the misery of those in this world,
Their sadness becomes mine.

RYŌKAN

Those who are possessed by desire suffer much and enjoy little, as the ox that drags a cart gets but a morsel of grass. For the sake of this morsel, which falls easily to the beast's lot, man, blinded by his destiny, wastes this brief fortune that is so hard to win.

SHANTIDEVA

Even on the morning of one's day of birth, omens of death appear;
Be ever alert and watchful; waste no time. . . .
Ever transient is this world of ours; all things change and pass away.
For a distant journey even now prepare.

PADAMPA SANGYE

When Fa-hsien* was in India, it made him sad to see a fan from his native land and, when he lay sick, he longed for Chinese food. Some-

---

* The celebrated monk (*fl.* 399–414) who spent ten years in India and returned to China with many texts of Buddhism, which he translated from Sanskrit into Chinese.

13

one who heard this story remarked, 'To think that so eminent a man should have let people in a foreign country see how terribly weak-spirited he was.' But the Abbott Kōyū answered, 'How touchingly human of him.'

KENKŌ

Living beings are helpless, wrapped up in sickness.

Avataṃsaka Sūtra

Whatever occurs, we in our foolishness can keep our composure only so long as we avoid facing it squarely. Our aspiration may appear imposing but, if something happens, it is easily shaken.

MYŌZEN

The great glories of this world pass away in the twinkling of an eye.

T'U LUNG

The best knowledge is that which enables one to put an end to birth-and-death, and to attain freedom from the world.

Khuddaka Nikāya

Our life is circumscribed by the actual changing physical world, while our inmost nature is always aspiring after the Absolute. Insurmount-able contradictions exist in our very essence.

RYUCHI FUJII

Man *is* his karma in the sense that all the various elements that together have gone into the composition of his empirical personality, what he and others take for his 'self', are one and all products of karma, and so are the modifications through which that personality passes in the course of its becoming: family, possessions, occasional happenings, illness, old age, or what you will. Apart from these 'acci-dental' products of becoming, that personality would not exist and, when they fall apart, it no longer is.

MARCO PALLIS

In the ocean of *saṃsāra*, the great culprit is the impermanent physical
   body;
Busy in its craving search for food and dress,
From worldly works it never finds relief. . . .

WHERE WE FIND OURSELVES

Amid the city of impermanent physical forms, the great culprit is the
unreal mind;
Submissive to the form of flesh and blood,
It never finds the time to realise the nature of Reality.

MILAREPA

Who can say with certainty that one will live to see the morrow?

The Ocean of Delight for the Wise

Us monks are said to overcome the realm of life and death;
Yet I cannot bear the sorrow of parting.

RYŌKAN

Joy, anger, grief and pleasure are all empty delusions but who does
not give themselves to them as if they were real?

KENKŌ

If you want to know the karmic causes which belong to the past, look
at the karmic effects which belong to the present. If you want to see
the karmic effects as they will appear in the future, look well to the
causes operating here and now.

Ingwa Sūtra

To what shall I compare this world?
To the white wake behind
A ship that has rowed away at dawn.

MANSEI

All worldly pursuits have but one unavoidable and inevitable end,
which is sorrow; acquisitions end in dispersion, buildings in destruction, meetings in separation; births in death. Knowing this . . . one
should set about realising the truth.

MILAREPA

We are urged to consider that nothing in our empirical self is worthy
of being regarded as the real self.

EDWARD CONZE

The objects of sense in the world ever changing—these we adhere to
as things of reality; but, in the ocean of birth-and-death, they drown

us. How long shall we wander down this path? This world to us indeed seems permanent and fixed. Yet, after all, what is it but a road of dreams to which, life after life, we must perforce return?

Zeami Motokiyo

Sentient beings are blind, ignorant and suffering . . . confused, always going in circles.

Avataṃsaka Sūtra

Life and death, past and present—
Marionettes on a toy stage.
When the strings are severed,
Behold the broken pieces.*

Unknown Zen Master

The world, as a whole, is hard to live in; both we and our dwellings are precarious and uncertain things. Moreover, in countless instances, we encounter further perplexities because of the places in which we live or our station in life.

Kamo no Chōmei

For the person who actually wants to attain the world beyond, nothing is more pointless than withdrawal from ordinary life.

Myōzen

As we receive birth, suffering is laden upon suffering, and each time we return to death, we make our way from darkness into further darkness. . . . Should we call this cycle of transformations in birth-and-death dream or reality? When we think to say it exists, it rises in clouds and vanishes like smoke; there is no one who keeps their shadowy form in the vacant sky. When we think to say it does not really exist, we still find, lodged within our hearts, grief at separation from ones we loved that never fails to cut to the bowels and leave the soul distraught.

Ippen

* "When life comes to an end, the illusions of this world also break into pieces." (Donald Keene)

WHERE WE FIND OURSELVES

The proud ones do not last long and their glory is like a spring night's dream. And the mighty ones too will ultimately perish, like dust before the wind.

The Tale of the Heike

In all things, it is the beginnings and the ends that are interesting. Does the love between men and women refer only to the moments when they are in each other's arms? The man who grieves over a love affair broken off before it was fulfilled, who bewails empty vows, who spends long autumn nights alone, who lets his thoughts wander to distant skies, who yearns for the past in a dilapidated house—such a man truly knows what love means.

KENKŌ

How can there be laughter, how can there be pleasure, when the whole world is burning? When you are in deep darkness, will you not ask for a lamp?

The Dhammapada

The irascible minds of all sentient beings,
Their bondage and ignorance, are as deep as the sea.

Avataṃsaka Sūtra

If we give thought to the matter, we would find that the self we think we know is only apparitional; the real self is something of which we know nothing. For this reason, we float through life in a dream; we deceive ourselves, thinking it our fate to paddle about, never reaching solid ground. Clinging to wife and child out of attachment to dear life, we strive to extend our life as long as possible. . . . We want to believe that we harbour, deep within ourselves, the light of inner convictions to see us through bad times.

But religion challenges our notions, saying: *Be yourself, throw down that mask, reflect on who you really are.* For those who truly wish to live, this is what must be done: admit the vanity of your knowledge and deeds, and confront the darkness and ignorance within you. Own up to the fact that, in an ever-changing world, we are merely life forms that bear within ourselves the terrible seed of our own demise. When it comes our time to confront this ultimate source of despair, there is no turning to family or worldly possessions for consolation.

At this final impasse we learn the truth that man, born alone, dies alone.

Forced to face the darkness of our own soul, there is one thing this miserable portrait of the self elicits from us: the desire to be saved.

DAIEI KANEKO

Like a fish that is thrown on dry land, taken from its home in the waters, the mind strives and struggles to get free from the power of Death.

The Dhammapada

All sentient beings suffer grief and fear.

Avataṃsaka Sūtra

The mortal who thinks of his gains or his honours, or the favour of many men, will be afraid of death when it falls upon him. Whatsoever it be in which the pleasure-crazed spirit takes its delight, that thing becomes a pain a thousand times greater. Therefore, the wise man will seek not for pleasure, for from desire arises terror.

SHANTIDEVA

A hundred years of living is but a transient moment, the length of which resembles a spark struck from a stone. The fate of life is like a bubble floating on water. Those who know nothing but income, fame and rank, will soon see their faces turning pale and their bodies degenerating. The gain of money is capable of filling valleys; however, this impermanent possession cannot purchase the things which do not come back.*

CHANG PO-TUAN

There are the noble and the lowly, but suffering is something that afflicts both in ample quantity. The poor and the wealthy cannot

---

* A comparable view is found in the Roman Stoic philosopher, Seneca (4 BCE–65 CE): "Nothing is durable, whether for an individual or for a society; the destinies of men and cities alike sweep onwards. Terror strikes amid the most tranquil surroundings and, without any disturbance in the background to give rise to them, calamities spring from the least expected quarter."

be said to be the same, but they are identical as far as not being free from distress.

ZONKAKU

We are helpless before time
Which ever speeds away.
And pains of a hundred kinds
Pursue us one after another. . . .
This is the way of the world;
And, cling as I may to life,
I know no help.

YAMANOUE NO OKURA

An enemy can hurt an enemy, and a man who hates can harm another man; but a man's own mind, if wrongly directed, can do him far greater harm.

The Dhammapada

He who would misuse the boon of human life is far more stupid than he who would employ a gold vessel inlaid with precious gems as a receptacle for filth.

NĀGĀRJUNA

Possessing power, a man is filled with greed and desire; lacking supporters, he is an object of contempt. Riches bring manifold fears, poverty finds one seething with discontent. Depend upon others and you become their creature; have dependents of your own to look out for, and love and obligation ensnare you. If you abide by the world's ways, you suffer the loss of freedom; if you flout them, you are looked on as mad. In what place can you live, what activities can you pursue, in order to ensure a haven for your body and bring even a moment of peace to your mind?

KAMO NO CHŌMEI

The warm family relations maintained between mother and child, and those closest to us, are of the sort that we should nurture but they exist only because the past karma we bear inside us allows them to exist; when the time comes for us to leave our loved ones behind, we have no choice but to cast off those ties and depart. When the time has run out for those karmic ties, although we may wish to stay close to our loved ones and want to be taken along, our wishes are not granted. . . . Though you meet someone with whom you want to live your whole life, when the karmic ties are severed you grow estranged and distant; though you meet someone of whom you are not especially fond, unless these karmic ties are exhausted, you may end up living your whole life in their company. All of this is due to past karmic causes and conditions, and is not just a matter of our life in this world.

SHINRAN

My noble father . . . has left no trace of ever having lived; my fond and loving mother is now nought but a heap of whitened bones. Even these are pictures of illusoriness which make me seek the contemplative life.

MILAREPA

Sentient beings are bound and covered by habitual delusion—
Conceited, careless, their minds run wild. . . .
Sentient beings lack wisdom,
Wounded and poisoned by the thorns of craving.

Avataṃsaka Sūtra

Zen is to have the heart and soul of a little child.

TAKUAN

The hour of death waits not its turn. Death does not necessarily come from the front; it may stealthily be planning an attack from behind. Everyone knows of death, but it comes unexpectedly, when people feel that they still have time, that death is not imminent. It is like the dry flats that stretch far out into the sea, only for the tide suddenly to flood over them onto the shore.

KENKŌ

'These are my sons. This is my wealth.' In this way, the fool troubles himself. He is not even the owner of himself: how much less of his sons and his wealth!

The Dhammapada

We cannot trust in anything. The foolish man places great trust in things, and this sometimes leads to bitterness and anger. If you have power, do not trust in it; powerful men are the first to fall. You may have many possessions, but they are not to be depended on; they are easily lost in a moment. . . . Nor should you trust in another person's kind feelings; they will certainly change. Do not rely on promises; it is rare for people to be sincere. If you trust neither in yourself nor in others, you will rejoice when things go well, but bear no resentment when they go badly.

KENKŌ

Dew drops of birth-and-death vanish forever. Man's body is left to rot in field or forest, and bones bleach on some remote mountain to become, at last, a mere heap of dust covered in moss or grass while, under open skies, the spirit wanders alone. Wife, children and family, who dwell together where once he dwelt, cannot comfort him. Far from him is his treasure-house full of precious things. Regret and bitterness are his companions.

HŌNEN

Forever it has been that mourners, in their turn, were mourned.

Old Chinese Poem

Eager to escape sorrow, people rush into sorrow; from desire of happiness, they blindly slay their own happiness, enemies to themselves.

SHANTIDEVA

Rare it is to be born in human form, yet we take the lives of other living things to satisfy our craving for the taste of flesh, this being something that we should never do, and even the Buddha thus sets forth strict precepts against it. However, sentient beings of the present age in this defiled world live in a time without precepts, such that there are neither those who hold them nor those who violate them. As a result, although my head is shaved and I wear the dyed robes of a priest, because my heart is identical to those of the ordinary worldly masses, I eat things like this. Ah, if only this massive urge to eat could, instead, be converted into the work of liberating these living things.

SHINRAN

But death, the end of all, carries away the man who—ever thirsting for desires—gathers the flowers of sensuous passions, even as a torrent of rushing water overflows a sleeping village, and then runs forward on its way.

The Dhammapada

Let us control ourselves and not be resentful when others disagree with us, for we all have hearts and each heart has its own leanings. The right of others is our wrong, and our right is their wrong. We are not unquestionably sages, nor are they unquestionably fools. Both of us are simply ordinary people. How can anyone lay down a rule by which to always distinguish right from wrong? For we are all wise, sometimes, and foolish at others. Therefore, although others give way to anger, let us on the contrary dread our own faults, even though we may think we alone are in the right.

PRINCE SHŌTOKU

We are eternally swayed by the pleasing or displeasing circumstances around us, thanks to our constant preoccupation with pleasure and pain. Pleasure is liking and loving. We never cease our pursuit of this happiness. The pleasure we desire first of all is that of fame. There are two kinds of fame: glory derived from one's conduct, or from one's talents. The next pleasure desired is that of lust, the third of appetite. None of our other desires can equal these three. They arise from a perverted view of life and cause innumerable griefs. It is best not to seek them.

KENKŌ

Do not permit the events of your daily life to bind you, but never withdraw yourselves from them.

HUANG PO

Somebody asked Jōshū: 'The Buddha is the enlightened one and teacher of us all. He is naturally free of all passions, is he not? Jōshū said: 'No, he is the one who cherishes the greatest of all passions.' 'How is this possible?' 'His greatest passion is to save all beings!' Jōshū answered.

Traditional Zen Story

Karmic evil is from the beginning without real form;
It is the result of delusional thought and invertedness.

WHERE WE FIND OURSELVES

Mind-nature is from the beginning pure,
But as for this world, there is no person of truth.

SHINRAN

There is a vast preponderance of those who wander downwards
unliberated.

The Tibetan Book of the Dead

Few cross the river of time and are able to reach *Nirvāṇa*. Most of
them run up and down only on this side of the river.

The Dhammapada

Alas, people are busily engaged in secular matters,
Taking no notice of their lives wearing away by day and by night,
Like a lamp in the wind—how long can it last?
In the vast realms of *saṃsāra*, there is no fixed abode.
Until we are emancipated from the sea of suffering,
How can we rest peacefully? Why should we not be terrified?
Let us seek the path to Eternity. . . .
Impermanence rushes upon me at every moment;
The King of Death follows me in every step.
Let me urge you, practitioners of the Way,
To strive diligently to attain *Nirvāṇa*. . . .
Man's life, if wasted in idleness,
Is like a plant without roots
Or like a cut flower placed in the sun;
How long can it remain fresh?
Man's life is like this. Impermanence may seize you at any moment.
I urge you all . . . to attain Truth.

SHAN-TAO

They flock together like ants, hurry east and west, run north and
south. Some are mighty, some humble. Some are aged, some young.
They have places to go, houses to return to. At night, they sleep, in the
morning they get up. But what does all this activity mean? There is no
ending to their greed for long life, their grasping for profit. What
expectations have they that they take such good care of themselves?
All that awaits them in the end is old age and death, whose coming is
swift and does not falter for one instant. What joy can there be while

waiting for this end? The man who is deluded by fame and profit does not fear the approach of old age and death because he is so intoxicated by worldly cravings that he never stops to consider how near he is to his destination. The foolish man, for his part, grieves because he desires ever-lasting life and is ignorant of the law of universal change.*

KENKŌ

The world is no place to sit back and relax; it is precisely a burning house, filled with suffering, and those who live within its walls should hold it in the greatest of fear.

Abhidharma-kośa

In the world, many dwell in transitory abodes
Without knowledge of the land beyond.

PRINCE SHŌTOKU

We start dying the moment we are born. . . . Birth is the cause of death. All the circumstances which may bring about actual death are but its occasions. The act of birth, or conception to be more accurate, is the decisive cause which makes death inevitable. . . . We are all the time aware of our perilous condition, whether we dare face it or not. How *can* one be at one's ease in the interval?†

EDWARD CONZE

It is hard to keep this body together, like a scarecrow of leaves swept

---

* A view echoed by the famed Greek tragedian, Sophocles (496–406 BCE) over 1,700 years earlier: "A man who is desperate for long life and willingly prolongs his grief for more than a man's span of years is a fool to his last breath. For what does old age bring but biting pains, bitter tears and pleasures few and decreased? Sooner or later, the same death, not with marriage songs but funeral weeping, delivers us all to the earth. Not to be born is best. But, having been born, the next best thing is to return to the place from which one has come: our beginning and end. Youth soon passes like a carnival of frivolity. Horror and pain follow behind realities bleak and inescapable. Greed, envy, rapine, civil war and carnage: old age only increases the torment. Short of friends and breath, you struggle on towards the last crisis."
† Conze continues: "I sometimes believe that the English persisted in the gentle habit of executing criminals by hanging, because this form of execution affords such a close parallel to the course of human life. At the moment of conception we jump, as it were, off a board with a noose around our necks. In due course, we will be strangled—it is only a matter of sooner or later."

up by the wind; how quickly this life vanishes like dew on the grass! Mourning in the southern quarter, mourning in the north village, there is no stopping the stream of tears as we send off our loved ones. In the hills there are funerals, on the plains there are funerals, the soil being turned over so often to receive their bones that it has no chance to dry. How painful it is to think that, once they breathe their last, we must mourn for our dearest friends. Even the unbreakable bonds of intimate relationships are such that when a soul must go its way, we have no choice but to mourn our loss alone.

JŌKEI

The old adage has it: 'When the dragon has soared to the summit, it knows the chagrin of descent.' The moon waxes only to wane; things reach their height only presently to decline. In all matters, the principle holds true that decline threatens when further expansion is impossible.

KENKŌ

Was it yesterday you were kneeling by the burial mound, wiping away the tears you shed? Or is it tonight you are to send off another, as you break down and weep by the coffinside? So it is that for transients like us, an entire lifetime comes to pass . . . a phantasm as it were. It slips away quickly and, of the faces we see among us today, there is none who will remain a hundred years from now. I might be first to go, you might be first to go; it can happen today, it can happen tomorrow— who can tell? Whether you are left behind or not, sooner or later we all pass on like the incessantly vanishing dew.

EMPEROR GO-TOBA

All sentient beings are shrouded by afflictions,
Roaming in all conditions, subject to all miseries. . . .

Avataṃsaka Sūtra

We may take, for example, the life of a man who, let us say, has accumulated good karma throughout a long life, a man cared for by many children and grandchildren who one day enjoy the flower festival and, on another day, gather to view the moon. They love him dearly with deep filial piety so that others envy him and say: 'What a happy man he must be!' But even though he may be happy in this way, still in accordance with the law of the impermanence of things, this happiness cannot last. If one or two of his children die, he is saddened because they precede him in death and his long life becomes a burden to him. Henceforth, he sheds the tears of old age. His body gradually declines in strength and, at last, becomes a vehicle of impermanency, and he is made a lonely man. He continues to feel sad. Wealth may fill his coffers and he may have a magnificent house with a roof facing east and west and with a far view towards the north and south. A pleasant song . . . and the sunshine of spring may charm him. He may be entertained by the dancing of beautiful women whose long sleeves are spread out by the breezes, or he may be fascinated with the autumn scenery; yet all these things pass away with time, the man changes and all becomes but as a dream of yesterday.

GENSHIN

Jealousy, haughtiness and indolence . . . arise from stupidity;
With the fire of anger and malevolence
I have always burnt the good roots of wisdom and compassion.

SHAN-TAO

The mind of an ordinary person is never at rest but ceaselessly chases after sensory stimulation, like a monkey leaping from branch to branch of a tree. Perpetually distracted, the mind is very easy to stir up and very hard to calm down.

HŌNEN

It is easy to see the faults of others but difficult to see one's own. One shows the faults of others like chaff winnowed in the wind, but one conceals one's own faults as a cunning gambler conceals his dice.

The Dhammapada

The flowers of the spring fall beneath the branches;
Dew in autumn vanishes before the withered grass.
Flowing water can never be stopped;
Whirling winds howl constantly.
The world of senses is a sea in which one may well drown;
Eternity, Bliss, the Self* and Purity are the summits on which we
    ultimately belong.

KŪKAI

* This is a reference to the universal 'Self' (Buddha-nature) that is one in all sentient beings, not our individual egos.

WHERE WE FIND OURSELVES

Desire becomes a source of danger only when the object is such as to give no lasting satisfaction when it is attained.

CAROLINE RHYS DAVIDS

Harmony should be valued and quarrels should be avoided. Everyone has their biases and few of us are far-sighted.

PRINCE SHŌTOKU

All beings are shrouded in the great darkness of ignorance,
Burnt by the fire of lust and hate. . . .
Completely bound by the ropes and chains of craving,
Made desolate by the wastelands of deceit.

Avataṃsaka Sūtra

I (Buddha) see wandering beings who are poor, deprived of merit
   and wisdom;
Who are entering into the bitter path of birth-and-death,
And are suffering repeatedly and without end.
They are deeply attached to the desires of the five senses,
Just as yaks are attached to their tails. . . .
Deeply immersed in false views,
They try to eliminate suffering through suffering.
I feel great compassion
For such sentient beings. . . .
The Buddha teaches *Nirvāṇa*
To people with dull faculties. . . .
Who are attached to the realm of birth-and-death. . . .
And are perplexed by suffering.
Having devised skillful means
I enable them to enter the wisdom of the Buddhas.

Lotus Sūtra

The human body is transient, weak, impotent, frail and mortal. An intelligent person never places their trust in such a thing; it is like a bubble that soon bursts. It is like a mirage which appears because of a thirsty desire. It is like a plantain tree which is hollow on the inside. It is like a phantom caused by a conjurer. It is like a dream giving false ideas. . . . It is like a floating cloud which changes and vanishes. It is like the lightning which instantly comes and goes. . . . It has no

27

durability as the wind has none. . . . It is false and will be reduced to nothingness, in spite of bathing, clothing or nourishment. It is a calamity and subject to a hundred and one diseases. It is like a dry well threatened by decay. . . . To look upon the body as transient and sorrowful, empty and selfless; this is said to be wisdom.[*]

Vimalakīrti Sūtra

There is no fire like lust and there are no chains like those of hate. There is no net like illusion and no rushing torrent like desire.

The Dhammapada

Search into your self: but froth on a stream—
Once vanishing, nothing human remains.
Ponder your life and its shimmer of the moon,
Unstaying through rise and fall of each fleeting breath.
The smelling of fragrances, the tasting of tastes
Are for but a brief span;
When breath's manipulations have come to a halt,
No powers remain to this self. From far, far in the distant past,
Down to this day, this very instant,
Those things we have longed for most
Have not been attained, and we sorrow.
With minds that have deviated completely from the truth
We consider wrong and right to be one.
This insight is darkness; how shameful it is!

IPPEN

We cannot hold on forever to those whom we love, to things we want, to the fame and fortune we have; in the end, we must part from all these. How empty the years seem as our life dwindles to a close. Think it through for yourself: even world-conquering kings cannot hold on to their high status and many treasures forever. . . .[†] Although we

---

[*] "The body in itself is not to be devalued or denied, for it is the indispensable vehicle for the human spirit. Condemnation of the body is only valid when it is considered as the seat of the passions or as a provisional method when the aspirant needs to become detached from bodily demands." (Harold Stewart)

[†] The Greek dramatist, Menander (342–290 BCE), once wrote: "If you want to find out who you are, study the graves you encounter as you pass them by. Inside are the bones and fine dust of kings, of tyrants, of the wise and of men who were proud of

confront this kind of truth, we only pretend to understand it. Inured to a life hemmed in by desires, the ordinary person is not in the least astonished by the law of impermanence. Ah, how empty we ordinary persons are!

ZONKAKU

When I see the things people do in their struggle to get ahead, it reminds me of someone building a snowman on a spring day, making ornaments of precious metals and stones to decorate it.... How often it happens that a man continues to struggle in the hope of some success, even as the life left to him is melting away, like a snowman, from underneath.

KENKŌ

Despising the oceans of birth-and-death,
I yearn for a highland free from tides.

PRINCE SHŌTOKU

My observation of people leads me to conclude, generally speaking, that even those with some degree of intelligence are likely to go through life supposing they have ample time before them. But would a man, fleeing because a fire has broken out in his neighbourhood, say to the fire, 'Wait a moment please!'? To save his life, a man will run away, indifferent to shame, abandoning his possessions. Is a man's life any more likely to wait for him? Death attacks faster than fire or water, and is harder to escape. When its hour comes, can you refuse to give up your parents, your little children and your affections for others because they are hard to abandon?

KENKŌ

Deranged men do not perceive their madness; the blind are unaware of their blindness.
Born, reborn and still born again; whence they have come, they do not know.
Dying, dying and dying yet again; where they go in the end, they do not know.

their noble descent, their wealth, their glory and the beauty of their bodies. Not one of these things protected them against time. All mortals come to the same end. Look toward these to know who you are."

Deranged men wrongly believe in the notion of a permanent ego and
are firmly attached to it.
They rush around like thirsty deer seeking water in a dusty field,
believing mirages to be real.

KŪKAI

The world is afflicted with death and decay; therefore the wise do not
grieve, knowing the terms of the world.*

Khuddaka Nikāya

What is there in this world that should be longed for? What pleasure
is there that ought to be sought after? . . . In the same family, when
one of the parents, children, brothers, sisters, husband or wife dies,
those surviving mourn over the loss and their attachment to the
deceased persists. Deep sorrow fills their hearts and, grief-stricken,
they mournfully think of the departed. Days pass and years go by, but
their distress goes on. Even if someone teaches them the Way, their
minds are not awakened. Brooding over fond memories of the dead,
they cannot rid themselves of attachment. Being ignorant, inert and
illusion-bound, they are unable to think deeply, to keep their self-
composure . . . and to distance themselves from worldly matters. As
they wander here and there, they come to their end and die before
entering the Way. What, then, can be done for them?

Sūtra on the Buddha of Immeasurable Life

The whole earth cannot satisfy the lust of the flesh; who can do its
will? To those who long for the impossible, come guilt and bafflement
of desire.

SHANTIDEVA

---

* "The Buddhist seeks for a total happiness beyond this world. Why should he be
so ambitious? Why not be content with getting as much happiness out of this world
as we can, however little it may be? The answer is that, in actual practice, we are not
seen to be content. If an increase in physical comfort and earthly satisfactions
would make us so, then the inhabitants of the suburbs of London should be
immeasurably more radiant and contented than Chinese coolies or Spanish peas-
ants. The exact opposite is the case. Our human nature, according to the Buddhist
contention, is so constituted that we are content with nothing but complete permanence, complete ease and complete security. And none of that can we ever find in
this shifting world." (Edward Conze)

WHERE WE FIND OURSELVES

When I deeply contemplate the transient nature of human existence, I realise that, from beginning to end, life is impermanent like an illusion.... How fleeting is a lifetime! Who in this world today can maintain a human form for even a hundred years? There is no knowing whether I will die first or others, whether death will occur today or tomorrow. We depart one after another more quickly than the dewdrops on the tips of the blades of grasses. So it is said. Hence, we may have radiant faces in the morning but, by evening, we may turn into white ashes. Once the winds of impermanence have blown, our eyes are instantly closed and our breath stops forever. Then, our radiant face changes its colour and its attractive countenance, like peach and plum blossoms, is gone. Family and friends will gather and grieve, but to no avail. Since there is nothing else that can be done, they carry the deceased out to the fields, and then what is left after the body has been cremated and turned into midnight smoke is just white ashes. Words fail to describe the sadness of it all. Thus the ephemeral nature of human existence is such that death comes to young and old alike without discrimination.*

RENNYO

All philosophies in the world are but mental fabrications;
There has never been a single doctrine
By which one could enter the true essence of things.

Avataṃsaka Sūtra

No matter who it is, no one stays forever here in this fleshy body. The only difference is that either I myself or someone else must be left behind while the other goes ahead. Then, if we think of the period of time that will separate us, that too is uncertain. And even though they may call it long, at the longest it is only like a short dream or vision.

HŌNEN

Living to do the things we plan for the day and for the morrow, attached to life's pleasures and refusing to look suffering in the eye, we

---

* A sentiment expressed somewhat more vividly by the German philosopher, Arthur Schopenhauer (1788–1860): "We begin in the madness of carnal desire and the ecstasy of sensual pleasure; we end in the dissolution of all our parts and the musty stench of corpses."

never notice the demon, Death, encroaching. Busied with everything else, we never even notice the days and nights passing by in a blur.

ZONKAKU

If you have an eyelash and place it in the palm of your hand, you cannot feel it. If that eyelash were put in your eye, though, it would cause pain and you cannot be at rest. It is said that the foolish, like the palm, do not know what suffering is; while the wise, like the eye, having been touched by the eyelash of suffering, have a great loathing and fear of it.

Abhidharma-kośa

It is painful to leave the world; it is painful to be in the world; and it is painful to be alone amongst the many. The long road of transmigration is one of pain for the traveller: let them rest by the road and be free.

The Dhammapada

At the horrible time of the end, men will be malevolent, false, wicked and obtuse and they will imagine that they have reached perfection when it will be nothing of the sort.

Lotus Sūtra

Common hearts of the defiled world, possessed of both the clever and fools alike, cannot be said to be very different.

ZONKAKU

Sentient beings are shrouded in darkness,
Sunk in eternal night.
Buddha preaches truth for them, bringing the dawn.

Avataṃsaka Sūtra

A certain hermit once said: 'There is one thing that even I, who have no worldly entanglements, would be sorry to give up—the beauty of the sky.' I can understand why he should have felt that way.[*]

KENKŌ

---

[*] "For Kūkai (founder of the Shingon school), what is beautiful partakes of the Buddha." (E. Dale Saunders, *Buddhism in Japan*, p. 161)

WHERE WE FIND OURSELVES

All the pleasant things of the world
Are born of the Buddha....
All virtuous activities in the world
Come from the Buddha's light.

Avataṃsaka Sūtra

If we were never to fade away ... never to vanish ... but lingered on
forever in the world, how things would lose their power to move us.

KENKŌ

I swoon, intoxicated
By the sweet scent of jasmine on a summer's night
And the ecstatic trill of cicadas.
To think that the Buddha's blissful light reaches me even here;
In this beguiling garden of *saṃsāra.*

JŌKŌ

Midnight.
Everybody in the house is sleeping,
Even the hourglass has stopped.
But I cannot sleep.
Because the trembling spring flowers,
Whose shadow the moon throws against the wall,
Are more beautiful than what a man can bear.

WANG AN-SHIH

CHAPTER TWO

ULTIMATE REALITY

—Source and Destination

Introduction

Most Buddhists in the West consider themselves thoroughly secular in their outlook. They would also say that religion has no role to play in their beliefs or practice. This is because they see Buddhism as a way of simply improving their lives through meditation, mindfulness and the observation of ethical precepts. The focus is very much on wholesome behaviour, a better understanding of our minds and emotions, and a desire to create a kinder, more harmonious world. All very laudable objectives and not in any way requiring, it seems, a belief in higher realities of a spiritual nature.

The history of the Buddhist tradition, however, confronts us with a very different picture. Here we find supernatural buddhas, transcendent beings, miraculous happenings, divine realms in other parts of the cosmos and so forth. We also find a rich variety of devotional practices along with inspiring stories of faith, wonder and joy. While meditation and the moral life were a central feature of Buddhism as well, this traditional view is clearly more complex and diverse than the, arguably, one-dimensional variety of it that is dominant in some quarters today. How do we account for this disparity?

On one level, it is clear that our beliefs are fundamentally moulded by prevailing ideological currents through which traditional spiritual forms are filtered and modified. Many people in the modern world have little tolerance for the supernatural or metaphysical—indeed for anything that cannot be clearly demonstrated by empirical methods. We live in a largely faithless age where the reigning forces are science and economics. Therefore, it should come as no surprise that these dispositions are reflected in the Buddhism of today; especially when you consider that this tradition lends itself more readily to a multiplicity of beliefs which it appears to accommodate with great flexibility. Accordingly, it is very easy to cherry-pick those features that suit one's worldview.

However, there was a time (in fact during the greater portion of its long history) when Buddhist belief was permeated by powerful unseen realities that profoundly influenced people's lives and destinies. Life in this world was not seen as being the only one, nor was there the inordinate focus on the individual, as an end in itself, that we see today. While other spiritual traditions have also changed over time, none seem to display the variety of doctrines encompassed by Buddhism.

Notwithstanding this complex diversity and vastness of scale, there has always been a certain 'bedrock' set of beliefs without which Buddhism is no longer recognisable. Concepts such as *dharma*, *nirvāṇa* and *karma* are familiar to many (even if imperfectly understood). We will encounter more of these terms throughout this book but, chief among them, are those relating to the spiritual goal to which Buddhism (of all schools) aspires.

One of the challenges that seekers face is the elusive nature of this goal—a difficulty compounded by the many terms that are deployed to describe it. The reason it is designated in so many ways is because it is possible to approach it from a variety of angles and perspectives. Hence we find it referred to as Enlightenment, Buddhahood, *Nirvāṇa*, Suchness, *Bodhi*, Dharma-Body, *Tathāgata*, Buddha-Nature, Emptiness and so on. Let there be no doubt that all these terms are not describing fundamentally different things but one reality—a reality that is indubitably *spiritual*. This will become readily apparent in the passages that follow.

When considered in all its implications, this reality cannot be reduced to just an aspiration, a worldly virtue, a neurological event in our brains or even the highest manifestation of kindness or goodwill. It is a genuinely mysterious presence that lies at the heart of all things. The sages of the tradition tell us that it is the ultimate good, the highest reality, the true self, blissful, undefiled, the eye of wisdom, not prone to decay or impermanence, the ultimate source of existence, total liberation, the way things truly are, egoless realisation and the end to all suffering. When one reflects on the insights offered in this chapter, it becomes difficult to see this reality as anything other than an all-encompassing numinous realm that is utterly transcendent to our ordinary world but also, inconceivably, immanent in all things—wholly 'other' yet inseparable from everything at the same time. Any attempt to pin it down leads you to the very limits of language and, ultimately, to stark paradoxes. This is to be expected when trying to envelop something that resists our worldly logic and conventional frames of reference. You might ask why anybody would be inclined to believe in something so strange and perplexing; so fugitive and intangible, seeing as it runs counter to our ordinary understanding of things.

And, yet, the unquestionable experience of this reality has been so powerful and prevalent over the 2000 years of Buddhist history, commencing with the Buddha's own awakening, that every effort has been expended to capture it in words, however inadequate they may be. The very force and luminosity of this experience, which can also be ours, served to convince the authors of the following passages that encountering this reality was the most important quest in life and the only solution to the pressing plight of a humanity that is incomplete without it.

This reality is Enlightenment because it illumines the truth for us; it is *Nirvāṇa* because, in it, we find our deepest joy and happiness; it is 'Suchness' because it is the essence of all things; it is the Dharma-Body because it embraces everything in one living unity; and it is the 'Void' because it is empty of delusion, suffering and impermanence. Considered in this way, it represents the foundation of all Buddhism—its beginning and end—without which there can be no truth and no path to follow. It is not something the world can bestow and our awakening to it can be likened to being given a precious gift that can never be earned.

The Fragrance of Light

The Dharma is far above mere talk.

Vimalakīrti Sūtra

The expressible nature of things is not their true nature.

K'uei-Chi

Our original Buddha-nature is void,* omnipresent, silent, pure; it is a glorious and mysteriously peaceful joy.

Huang Po

The things I (Buddha) have directly known but have not taught you are numerous, while the things I have taught you are few.

Saṃyutta Nikāya

Buddha has reality for his body,
Pure as space itself;
All the physical forms that appear
He includes in this reality.

Avataṃsaka Sūtra

Throughout all the ten regions of the universe, there is no place where the Absolute is not.

Hakuin

---

* "It might seem as if, by the use of the term *Void*, we must imply quiescence or a static condition but, on the contrary, this 'void' is something which is really the veritable ground of the universe; it is dynamic like a bow at full stretch, ready to shoot an arrow, ever in a state of tense potential activity, evolving from within its bosom all the differentiations of the diversified phenomena of the world. Buddhists have an expression—*fushu jishō*—which means that the great 'void' of potentialities, of which we have been speaking, cannot preserve its undifferentiated state but, being dynamic, must be ever changing itself into the differentiated phenomena of the world as we know it. This word *Void* was chosen as the most fitting to help us get wholly free from the disconcerting illusions which seem inseparable from sense perceptions, the natural inferences from which are always in danger of beclouding the mind, by confining its attention to the external and temporary phases of passing phenomena. Reality can only be reached by rigidly rejecting such, one by one, leaving a great void or nothing whatever behind but the all-embracing timeless potentialities that must be postulated to account for the world at all." (Harper Havelock Coates & Ryugaku Ishizuka, *Honen the Buddhist Saint: His Life and Teachings*, pp. xii–xiii)

ULTIMATE REALITY

There is an unborn, unbecome, unmade and unconditioned; for were there not an unborn, unbecome, unmade and unconditioned, no escape could be discerned from what is born, become, made and conditioned.

Khuddaka Nikāya

The truth is that all things rise, exist, decay and die in accordance with the universal law of cause and condition. Things are real in the sense that they exist temporarily in a causal relation, but they are void in the sense that they have no permanent reality.... The ultimate source of all things, *Suchness,** must be considered empty in the sense that it transcends all thought and expression.

Ryuchi Fujii

The ultimate reality itself is not a symbol, it leaves no tracks; it cannot be communicated by letters or words, but we come to it by tracing them to the source from which they issue forth.

Hori Kintayu

From (Reality), which does not abide anywhere, springs the world and living beings.

Śūraṅgama Sūtra

It is identical with the essence of things, as it is immanent in them all.

Vimalakīrti Sūtra

---

* "Buddhism says that 'Suchness' (*tathatā* in Sanskrit) ... produces and unifies the universe. *The Awakening of Faith* clearly states that, as the ultimate ground of all things, it is not subject to increase or diminution but is permanent and, as the essential nature of the universe, it is possessed of all potentialities while, as a living active force, it produces all the phenomena of the secular and spiritual life of sentient beings. A famous passage which defines Suchness in this sense, reads thus: 'In its nature, it is always full of possibilities and is described as of great light and wisdom ... and knowing things as they really are. Its true nature is that of a pure mind, eternally joyful, the true soul of things, tranquil and immutable.' If we are asked if Suchness is endowed with personality, we at once reply 'certainly not' in the limited sense we speak of human personality but 'certainly yes' if we recognise it as endowed with all the foregoing absolute attributes." (Harper Havelock Coates & Ryugaku Ishizuka, *Honen the Buddhist Saint: His Life and Teachings*, pp. xiv–xv)

That which is beyond speech and conception pervades the entire universe.

KŪKAI

This world exists in terms of time and space and, consequently, changes and disappears. It is doomed to decay and destruction. Our ideal cannot be realised in this changing world but in the other world. Our hope and aspiration are in that eternal and immutable life.

RYUCHI FUJII

The multitude of living beings are included in the Buddha's Wisdom ... the Buddha's Body penetrates everywhere.

Ratnagotravibhāga

The Dharma-Body[*] ... is the perfection of permanence, the perfection of happiness, the perfection of the substantial self and the perfection of purity.

Sūtra of Queen Śrīmālā of the Lion's Roar

A Buddha is called an awakened one just because his knowledge owes nothing to the world or to the empirical ego that jointly provided the focus of his previous dreaming.

MARCO PALLIS

Reality must be intelligent, rational, moral, dynamic and energetic if it be truly of Wisdom and Compassion.

WASUI TATSUGUCHI

Just as there can be no ice without water, so *Nirvāṇa* is immediately present.

HAKUIN

---

[*] "*Suchness* may sound too abstract and metaphysical, and the *Mahāyāna* frequently substitutes 'Mind' for it; 'Mind' is a more familiar and, therefore, more accessible ... term for general Buddhists, who can thus establish an intimate relation between their individual minds and Mind as final reality. When, however, even 'Mind' is regarded as too intellectual, Buddhists call it *Dharmakāya* ('Dharma-Body') ... *kāya* is 'the body' more in the moral sense of 'person' or 'personality'. The *Dharmakāya* is, therefore, a person whose bodily, organic or material expression is this universe, *Dharma*." (D.T. Suzuki, *A Miscellany on the Shin Teaching of Buddhism*, p. 10)

ULTIMATE REALITY

The perception of a phenomenon is the perception of the Universal Nature, since phenomena and Mind are one and the same.

HUANG PO

All beings are of Suchness. All things too are of Suchness.

Vimalakīrti Sūtra

The picture is not in the colours ... the Principle transcends the letter.

Laṅkāvatāra Sūtra

When good sons and daughters abandon the body ... having parted from old age, illness and death, they realise the indestructible, eternal, unchanging and inconceivable ... Dharma-Body.

Sūtra of Queen Śrīmālā of the Lion's Roar

All existences, the entire range of phenomena, are of the One Mind* alone and nothing is excluded. All these manifold phases of existence are equally of the One Mind and none differs from it.

DŌGEN

Within the heart of everything, there is ultimate reality ... *Nirvāṇa* is the unextinct *dharma*; it is the supreme end ... it is not itself anything born. In truth, all things are, in their ultimate nature, *Nirvāṇa* itself.

NĀGĀRJUNA

I take refuge in That One
Who is the adamantine Life of all beings,
Transcendental, immaculate, causeless and infinite.

KŪKAI

The common source of all things and all individual consciousness must be Universal Mind. The Universal Mind is the Absolute Buddha and is called *Dharmakāya*.

RYUCHI FUJII

---

* "The full diversity of sentient experience and the experienced world—the subjective and the objective, the true and the false, the pure and the defiled, the latent and the manifest—is seen to rest upon, or to grow from, a common noetic source." (Robert M. Gimello, *Chih-yen and the Foundations of Hua-Yen Buddhism*, p. 411)

The intellect reflects something of the divine nature, it is true, but it does not go beyond being a reflection; it can never be taken for the original light.

D. T. Suzuki

The Dharma-Body is named 'cessation of suffering' and it is beginningless . . . unborn, undying, free from death; permanent, steadfast, calm, eternal; intrinsically pure and free from all defilements.

Sūtra of Queen Śrīmālā of the Lion's Roar

The principle of One Mind has two aspects. One is the aspect of Mind in terms of the Absolute (*tathatā*; 'Suchness') and the other is the aspect of Mind in terms of phenomena (*saṃsāra*; 'realm of birth-and-death'). Each of these two aspects embraces all states of existence. Why? Because these two aspects are mutually inclusive.*

The Awakening of Faith in the Mahāyāna

That which is absolutely empty (Suchness) is yet not empty [since] it manifests itself as a variety of phenomena and is nowhere fixed. Matter, which is not different from emptiness, unfolds itself as all phenomenal existences.

Kūkai

The True Mind is eternal, permanent, immutable, pure and self-sufficient . . . it is unborn and imperishable. It is only through illusions that all things come to be differentiated.

The Awakening of Faith in the Mahāyāna

When Buddhists declares all things to be empty (*śūnyatā*), they are not advocating a nihilistic view; on the contrary, they are assuming an ultimate reality which cannot be subsumed in the categories of logic. To proclaim the conditionality of things is to assert the existence of

---

* "Reality is conceived as the intersection of the Absolute order and the phenomenal order; therefore, it contains in itself both . . . at once. The Absolute is thought to be transcendental and yet is conceived as not being outside of the phenomenal. Again the phenomenal is thought to be temporal and yet is conceived as not being outside of the Absolute. In other words, they are ontologically identical; they are two aspects of one and the same Reality." (Yoshito Hakeda, *The Awakening of Faith*, p. 32)

something altogether unconditioned and transcendent of all determination. *Śūnyatā* may thus often be most appropriately rendered as
'the Absolute.' ... No limiting qualities are to be attributed to it; while
it is immanent in all concrete and particular objects, it is itself not at
all definable.

SHAKU HANNYA

It is profound, it is vast; it is neither self nor other . . . a state of perfect
bliss in which existence has its origin. . . . Here, Sun and Moon lose
their distinction.

SARAHA

When you hear me talk about the Void, do not fall into the idea of
vacuity.

HUI-NENG

The essence of Suchness knows no increase or decrease. . . . It was not
brought into existence in the beginning nor will it cease to be at the
end of time; it is eternal through and through. From the beginning,
Suchness in its nature is fully provided with all excellent qualities;
namely, it is endowed with the light of great wisdom, the qualities of
illuminating the entire universe, of true cognition and mind pure in
its self-nature; of eternity, bliss, Self and purity; of refreshing cool-
ness, immutability and freedom. . . . Though it has, in reality, all these
excellent qualities, it does not have any characteristics of differentiation; it retains its identity and is of one flavour. Suchness is solely
one . . . it is one without a second.

The Awakening of Faith in the Mahāyāna

Neither life nor death is any more real than empty space which a man
slashes with his cold blade.

SOSHUN

It is on account of our limited senses and finite mind that we have a
world of particulars which, as it is, is no more than a fragment of
absolute Suchness. And yet, it is through this fragmentary manifestation that we are finally enabled to reach the fundamental nature of
being in its entirety.

D.T. SUZUKI

The Dharma-Body . . . is not engendered by acts and passion but is powerful in manifesting itself in conditioned images.

ASAṄGA

The *Tathāgata** is eternally quiescent yet its transformations permeate the universe.

GISHIN

Religious faith . . . wants to grasp what is not conditioned by time and space; it wishes to take hold of what is behind historical facts. And this must be Reality transcending the polarisation of subject and object.

D. T. SUZUKI

The Great Space, being boundless and silent, encompasses ten thousand images [phenomena] in its life-force; the Great Sea, deep and still, embraces a thousand elements in a single drop. The All-Embracing One is the mother of all things.

KŪKAI

The *Tathāgata* abides in the supremely abiding self, in unholy conditions, in human and evil destinies, and in unchaste conditions.

ASAṄGA

If all things come from Suchness, the Buddha and all things are the same in their true essence; all must be real and true. From this point of view, the whole world is not only the manifestation of the Buddha, but the Buddha himself. The universe, as a whole, is a living Buddha. The universe, including all things, is to be considered the body of Buddha . . . the perfect harmony of earth, water, fire, air, space and consciousness. In other words, the Buddha consists of mental and physical elements.

RYUCHI FUJII

* "A synonym for Buddha. The term is derived from combining *tathā-āgata*, which means to come from Suchness, or *tathā-gata*, to go to or arrive at Suchness. In East Asian Buddhism, the term *Tathāgata* is often used as a synonym for Buddha because of its dynamic connotations, expressed in particular in the sense that the *Tathāgata* 'comes from Suchness' . . ." (*The Collected Works of Shinran*, vol. 2, p. 210)

Foolish people ... assert that the five *skandhas** and other dharmas are definitely devoid of true existence.... However, to trace them back to their original substance, they are nothing but Suchness. For apart from the noumenal, the phenomenal has no separate nature.

K'UEI-CHI

The *Tathāgata's* Dharma-Body is possessed by all sentient beings ... and is able to carry them back to their origin.

WONHYO

We say that the Void has no inside or outside. There is only the spontaneously existing (Absolute). And, for this same reason, we say it has no centre.

HUANG PO

The Dharma-Body ... is beginningless, not distinct from [sentient beings] and infinite.

ASAṄGA

The Buddha-body is pure, ever calm,
Manifesting all forms, yet without any signs,
Abiding this way everywhere in the world.

Avataṃsaka Sūtra

In a world that has not been saved, a world without refuge, there is an inexhaustible, eternally-abiding refuge.

Sūtra of Queen Śrīmālā of the Lion's Roar

Śūnyatā is formless but it is the fountain-head of all possibilities.

D. T. SUZUKI

For the Bodhisattvas,† *Nirvāṇa* does not mean extinction.

Laṅkāvatāra Sūtra

---

* The psycho-physical elements of the individual; namely, matter, sensation, perception, mental formations and consciousness—the empirical ego as a transitory process; *dharmas* are the constituents of existence.

† *Bodhisattvas* ('enlightenment beings') are those who, out of great compassion, are dedicated to bringing others to spiritual emancipation and Buddhahood. They may be found either in our everyday midst, often in forms unbeknownst to us, or they can exercise their influence in this world from other realms.

Although it is Total Reality, there is no perceiver of it. How wondrous this is!

PADMASAMBHAVA

The true ideal world that is eternal, immutable and universal after which our souls aspire, as Plato claimed, must be beyond this changing world. . . . All things are manifestations of the absolute reality. . . . All is in one and one in all. Thus, the whole universe is the harmonious activity of the Universal Mind, the Absolute Buddha.

RYUCHI FUJII

I (Buddha) proclaim the Dharma eternally.

Lotus Sūtra

Sentient beings and Buddha-nature are not the same and, yet, they are not different.

WONHYO

All aspects of the universe—the relative and the absolute—are but one in reality.

HAKUIN

The essence of Suchness is, from the beginningless beginning, endowed with a perfect state of purity. It is provided with supra-rational functions and the nature of manifesting itself.

The Awakening of Faith in the Mahāyāna

The essence of reality is not empty.

K'UEI-CHI

The reality-body of the Buddha is inconceivable:
Colourless, formless, beyond any image,
Yet able to manifest a myriad forms for sentient beings.[*]

Avataṃsaka Sūtra

---

* The Hua-yen school, which was founded on this sutra, "sees all phenomena as expressions of an originally pure and undifferentiated one mind." (Jacqueline Stone, *Original Enlightenment and the Transformation of Medieval Japanese Buddhism*, p. 7)

Ignorance results from an unconscious and accidental estrangement from Suchness . . . it is the basic blindness lurking in the deepest level of the subconscious mind.

YOSHITO HAKEDA

All phenomena, without exception, are included in Suchness.

Avataṃsaka Sūtra

The purpose of stating that the *Dharmakāya* is 'quiescent, like empty space' is to negate the adherence to the notion that it is . . . a kind of anthropomorphic being among others in the universe. On the other hand, to believe that the *Dharmakāya* is literally 'non-being' is a wrong view.

YOSHITO HAKEDA

The dwelling of the *Tathāgata* is the great compassionate heart within all living beings.

Lotus Sūtra

Even when the Other is asked to come over to the self, it is not the self but the Other who makes the self move this way.

D. T. SUZUKI

If the essence of Mind ('Suchness') were to cease, then beings would be nullified and they would have no support.

The Awakening of Faith in the Mahāyāna

Buddha—an essence of immeasurable, incomprehensible, unfathomable . . . qualities and activities extremely wondrous—is vast like space and the holy source giving rise to all that is wished for by sentient beings.

DOLPOPA

The aim of Buddhism, like that of many other religions, is to gain immortality, a deathless life. The Buddha, after he had become enlightened, claimed to have opened the *doors to the Undying*. It is obvious that there is a great difference between the perpetuation of this individuality on the one hand and immortality on the other. Immortality is just the opposite of this life, which is bound up with death and inseparable from it.... Immortality is therefore not a desire to perpetuate an individuality which is bought at the price of inevitable decay, but a transcending of this individuality.

EDWARD CONZE

All things are different in their causal relations but are the same in their true essence. Rain, hail, ice and snow are different manifestations under different conditions but are reduced to the same water under the same condition.

RYUCHI FUJII

The realm of the Buddha is boundless, immeasurable. . . .
The light of the Buddha has no end; it fills the cosmos, inconceivably.

Avataṃsaka Sūtra

The *Dharmakāya* . . . [is a spiritual existence] which is absolutely one; it is real and true, and forms the *raison d'être* of all beings; it is free from desires and compulsion, and stands outside the pale of our finite understanding.

ASAṄGA

What is conditioned is impermanent and what is impermanent is false and deceptive in nature. What is false and deceptive in nature is not true . . . and not a refuge.

Sūtra of Queen Śrīmālā of the Lion's Roar

The *Dharmakāya* is unhindered like great space, contains all phenomenal forms and is everlasting. It is the basis on which all existing things rest.

KŪKAI

We came from the Absolute Buddha, exist in him and return to him.*

RYUCHI FUJII

The term 'Suchness' (*tathatā*) is symbolic, it is an index to that which is transcendental; a provisional device of language on the conceptual

---

* In the Shingon school, this Buddha—known as *Mahāvairocana* ('Great Sun')—is the "centre of the cosmos . . . the point towards which all integration moves and from which the multiplicity of the phenomenal world comes into form." (E. Dale Saunders, *Buddhism in Japan*, p. 168)

plane used in an attempt to establish some sort of communication in a realm where all communication fails.

YOSHITO HAKEDA

Originally, there is only Suchness; then the outflow [of the world] appears while Suchness remains unchanged. It is like a snake transforming into a dragon without changing its scaly covering. . . . The primary nature of all forms is as boundless as the infinite body of universal space. . . . The *Dharmakāya* is the fundamental reality of all things. Names are created and applied to it expediently according to circumstances. The wisdom it possesses is inexhaustible. . . . It generates and creates all things. . . . It contains, and fully endows, infinite wisdom and knowledge. . . . Every dharma in the universe, no matter whether it is manifesting itself or going into dissolution, must ultimately return to Suchness.

The Tsung Ching Record

To be strictly consistent with the law of causality, all things and the world as a whole must come from Suchness. If all things are manifestations of Suchness, they must all share the same nature as it. . . . Thus, all things are founded in the Absolute Mind (*Dharmadhātu*) and are interdependent.

RYUCHI FUJII

The principle of Suchness within us is absolutely pure in its essential nature, but is filled with innumerable defilements.

The Awakening of Faith in the Mahāyāna

'True Wisdom' is the wisdom of realising True Reality. Because True Reality is without forms, true wisdom is unknowing. 'Unconditioned *Dharmakāya*' is the body of Dharma-Nature. Because Dharma-Nature is *Nirvāṇa*, *Dharmakāya* is formless. Because it is formless, there is no form which it cannot manifest.

T'AN-LUAN

Sentient beings are infinite
Yet Buddha guards them all in his thoughts.

Avataṃsaka Sūtra

The cessation of becoming is *Nirvāṇa*.

Saṃyutta Nikāya

All things in the physical universe, all thoughts awakened in the mind, and all attributes stem from the universal Buddha-Mind. They are valuable in that they mould and integrate our personality.

WASUI TATSUGUCHI

The Dharma-Body is formless and shapeless, unmanifested and inconceivable, unseen and indescribable, having no abode, non-arising and non-perishing. Such is the true Dharma-Body.

TAO-CH'O

The city of bliss, tranquil and uncreated . . . is ultimately free and peaceful. . . . Let us return! . . . Since innumerable aeons ago, we have been transmigrating . . . and nowhere has there been any pleasure; we hear only the voices of grief and sorrow. After this present lifetime has ended, let us enter the city of *Nirvāṇa*!

SHAN-TAO

The reality-body is like space;
Unobstructed, without differentiation.
Physical forms appear like reflections,
Manifesting myriad appearances.

Avataṃsaka Sūtra

I am the primordial being of all,
And am called the 'Support of the World.'

Mahāvairocana Sūtra

The manifestations of this principle are infinite in number. . . . Though raindrops are many, they are of the same water. Though rays of light are not one, they are of the same body.

KŪKAI

'Emptiness' does not mean non-existence [but that which is] . . . devoid of a distinct, absolute, independent, permanent, individual entity or being, as an irreducible component in a pluralistic world. . . . However, this negation does not exclude the possibility of

ULTIMATE REALITY

Suchness being seen from a different viewpoint with which one is not accustomed. Hence, there is room to present Suchness, if it is done symbolically, as replete with attributes.

YOSHITO HAKEDA

Tathāgata is the true and real. The true and real is boundless space. *Tathāgata* is also thus: non-arising, non-perishing, un-ageing, un-dying, indestructible and incorruptible; it is not a created exist-ence.... All created things are impermanent.... Buddha-nature is the uncreated ... the uncreated is the eternal.... The *Tathāgata* has definitely taught that the Buddha-body is uncreated ... and that all beings have Buddha-nature.... Although all sentient beings have Buddha-nature, because it is covered over by blind passions, they cannot see it.

Nirvāṇa Sūtra

Dharmakāya, being 'emptiness' itself and having no tangible bodily existence, has to embody itself in forms and is manifested as bamboo, as a mass of foliage, as a fish, as a man, as a Bodhisattva, as a mind. But these manifestations themselves are not the *Dharmakāya*, which is something more than forms or ideas or modes of existence.

D. T. SUZUKI

The myriad animate beings teeming with life—all have their origin. The myriad things flourishing in profusion—each returns to its root. Since there has never been anything that is without a root or origin, and yet has branches or an end, how much less could [humanity], the most spiritual among the ... powers [of the cosmos] be without an original source? ... Although the true nature constitutes the [ulti-mate] source of bodily existence, its arising must surely have a causal origin, for the phenomenal appearance of bodily existence cannot be suddenly formed from out of nowhere.... The vital force with which we are endowed, when it is traced all the way back to its origin, is the primal *pneuma** of the undifferentiated oneness; and the mind that arises, when it is thoroughly investigated all the way back to its source, is the numinous mind of the Absolute.

TSUNG-MI

---

* *yüan-ch'i*—a term used to denote a cosmogonic force.

Since the *Dharmakāya* is the essence of corporeal form, it is capable of appearing in [such] form because, from the beginning, corporeal form and Mind have been non-dual. . . . Since the essential nature of wisdom is identical with corporeal form, the essence of corporeal form which has yet to be divided into tangible forms, is called *Dharmakāya* pervading everywhere.

The Awakening of Faith in the Mahāyāna

The essential nature of the One Mind is originally existent, unproduced and without extinction.

KAKUBAN

The ultimate goal of each individual being is to realise the meaning of the oneness of all things, thus identifying self with all others. . . . If all things are mutually interrelated, thus making up a living whole, the Absolute Buddha is everything and nothing exists outside of the Buddha. Everything, no matter how small it may be, is as real as everything else.

RYUCHI FUJII

The Buddha-body is like space, inexhaustible—
Formless, unhindered, it pervades the ten directions
. . . And manifests in response to all sentient beings.

Avataṃsaka Sūtra

Absolute truth, indivisible space and intrinsic awareness are the primal Buddha . . . the permanent, stable, eternal, everlasting, all-pervasive essence of reality.

DOLPOPA

Since the essence of Suchness cannot be predicated, it is called 'emptiness'; but if someone takes it as literally true, they assume a position in nihilism, [an] extreme and false view.* Though Suchness defies predication, it can be suggested symbolically by such terms as 'compassion,' 'light' and 'life.'

YOSHITO HAKEDA

---

* "It is an erroneous adherence to the notion that the essence of Suchness is absolute nothingness" (Fa-tsang). "The very basis of Hua-yen thought seems to be a view of an Absolute which existed prior in time to a concrete world of things which

ULTIMATE REALITY

The impartial, signless body of true Suchness,
The pure reality-body of untainted light;
With knowledge and calm, with innumerable bodies,
It preaches the truth, adapting to all.

Avataṃsaka Sūtra

Buddhahood is the one truly intrinsic value.

WASUI TATSUGUCHI

We are told that *Nirvāṇa* is permanent, stable, imperishable, immovable, ageless, deathless and unborn; that it is power, bliss and happiness, the secure refuge, the shelter and the place of unassailable safety; that it is the real Truth and the supreme Reality; that it is the Good, the supreme goal and the one and only consummation of our life—the eternal, hidden and incomprehensible Peace.

EDWARD CONZE

Suchness as absolute is too remote, too abstract and its existence or non-existence seems not to affect us in our daily social life, inasmuch as it is transcendental. In order to enter into our limited consciousness, to become the norm of our conscious activities, to regulate the course of the evolutionary tide in nature, Suchness must surrender its 'splendid isolation', must abandon its absoluteness.

it became. There it was said that any phenomenal object is a mixture of the True and the false, or the Unconditioned and conditioned (of course, the sum total of all things is this same mixture). Taking up the absolute side of things, Fa-tsang says that it itself has two aspects. First, he says, it is immutable. This is not surprising because all religions claim immutability as the nature of the Absolute. What kind of Absolute would it be which changed like the ordinary things of the world? Being immutable, the Absolute is forever unmoved, pure, eternal, still and serene. This is, in fact, a common description of the Absolute in all *Mahāyāna* forms of Buddhism. However, Fa-tsang next says something which not only seems to contradict this statement but which also is very unusual in Buddhism; he says that moved by certain conditions, this pure, unmoved eternal Reality changes and appears as the universe of phenomenal objects. However, like the gold which has become the ring, the immutable Absolute remains immutable. Here the picture is apparently one of the emanation of the concrete universe from an immutable Absolute with the result that things are a mixture of the Absolute and the phenomenal." (Francis H. Cook, *Hua-yen Buddhism: The Jewel Net of Indra*, p. 94)

When Suchness thus comes down from its sovereign-seat in the realm of unthinkability, we have this universe unfolded before our eyes in all its diversity and magnificence. Twinkling stars inlaid in the vaulted sky; the planet elaborately decorated with verdant meadows, towering mountains and rolling waves; beasts wildly running through the thickets; the summer heavens ornamented with white fleecy clouds and, on earth, all branches and leaves growing in abundant luxury; the winter prairie destitute of all animation, only with naked trees here and there trembling in the dreary north winds; all these manifestations, not varying a hair's breadth of deviation from their mathematical, astronomical, physical, chemical and biological laws, are naught else than the work of Suchness in nature.

When we turn to human life and history, we have Suchness manifested in all forms of activity as passions, aspirations, imaginations, and intellectual efforts. It makes us desire to eat when hungry and to drink when thirsty; it makes the man long for the woman and the woman for the man; it keeps children in merriment and frolic; it braces men and women bravely to carry the burden of life.... In brief, all the kaleidoscopic changes of this phenomenal world, subjective as well as objective, come from the playing hands of Suchness.

D. T. SUZUKI

CHAPTER THREE

LIVING THE WAY

—Signposts to Emancipation

Introduction

We now descend from the metaphysical heights of the previous chapter and explore the world of behaviour, self-awareness and practice. The aim here is to stress the importance of *embodying* our beliefs; that is, of putting flesh on the bones of mere theoretical knowledge. Many of the observations to be found here are readily intelligible and do not require much by way of explanation or context. That said, however, the role of morality in living the Buddhist life calls for some brief considerations.

Although many sutras contain ethical injunctions, they are not being arbitrarily prescriptive about how we ought to conduct ourselves. What they represent is how an awareness of the Dharma ought to manifest itself in our everyday attitudes and actions towards others. In other words, how an awakening to the truth about the way things are may naturally permeate our hearts and minds in a way that makes an ethical life the complement of our intellectual understanding of reality. In this light, morality ought not to be envisaged as just a means of gaining something else (e.g. virtue, praise, salvation) but as an end-in-itself. Treating it as a mere instrument cheapens its significance and severs its bond from the deeper foundations that sustain its value.

As we shall see in the final chapter, our capacity to lead morally flawless lives is inherently limited. We rarely measure up to the exalted standards of behaviour demanded by the teachings of the Buddha yet our disappointing failures in this regard should not give rise to the disparaging of fine or worthy conduct just because our own resolve is weak. The ethical exhortations of the Dharma are crucial in ensuring that our lives are informed by compassion and a general regard for others. The world would, undoubtedly, be a very different place if our capacity for fulfilling such ideals were considerably less imperfect. And, yet, we may find that a self-conscious attempt to become better will often fail precisely because of the dominance of our 'self', which stands as an impediment to overcoming its own limitations. An honest assessment of who and what we are will lead us, surely, to a view of ourselves that is disconcerting to say the least. The testament of the sages included in this book provides ample confirmation of this truth.

When our level of self-awareness reaches a point where we are confronted by our minds full of 'snakes and scorpions', to quote one master, we may feel impelled to gradually surrender that self to a higher power which is able to transform us to the extent that we allow it to do so. By creating an opening to something greater than ourselves, the 'virtues' of this reality are able to break through the hard crust of our cold egos to infuse us with its light and warmth. This infiltration will then manifest itself (despite some strong resistance at first) in qualities of thought and action that are redolent of wisdom and compassion, which—for this very reason—do not have their origin in us.

This may seem too passive an approach but the decision to abandon the suffocating confines of 'me' and 'I' is a most active—and decisive—step to take. As a consequence, it can lead to natural, spontaneous and uncontrived acts of genuine kindness, gentleness and empathy even though—paradoxically—we remain 'foolish beings' afflicted by the 'blind passions' of greed, anger and ignorance. It is as if the light of the Buddha-Mind pierces through our sclerotic self, despite the myriad obstacles thrown up by the latter, so that it is able to shine in the world and declare its presence as that which is 'true and real.'

The moral dimension of life, therefore, should be viewed as the heart of this reality showing itself through the benevolent actions of human beings who become awakened to it. By recognising its embrace of us, we make possible the manifestation of this light through the broken vessel that constitutes ordinary human nature. In this way, we are able to establish an intimate connection between the Buddha and ourselves. An ethical perspective lacking this spiritual dimension cannot maintain its integrity for long.

Similarly, we find that the deeper meaning of compassion ('to bear or suffer with') rests on a profound metaphysical reality—the fundamental unity of all beings as manifestations or expressions of the ultimate reality that Buddhism knows as the Dharma-Body. This abiding spiritual connection which we share with all livings things is what enables us to experience sympathy and practice loving-kindness because, at heart, we are essentially one with this reality, even though we never fully experience this fact in our distracted and self-absorbed lives. The capacity to think of others and take their well-being into account—even if we are oblivious to what makes this possible—demonstrates the all-pervading and unhindered nature of the Buddha's light which seeks to dispel our darkness of mind and the hardness in our hearts. We thereby attain joy in the knowledge that, in submitting our better nature to the working of this light, we are partaking of a life that is eternal and the essence of everything that is good and true.

When the siren of a fire truck wails faraway and the sound disappears into the distance, you do not give it a second thought. But when the shrill sound of the siren approaches your neighbourhood, you listen intently with your whole being. They are the same siren, but the implications are a world apart. Now the words of the Buddha are like the sound of the siren coming your way and warning you of the perils of the unreflected life. You must listen to the teachings with the same sense of urgency and involvement you show in listening to the cry of the approaching siren in the midnight air. Then, the message of the Buddha will become a part of you and you will open the eyes of your heart to reality, serenity and fullness.

GYODO HAGURI

The practice of Dharma consists in having kindness, generosity, truthfulness, purity, gentleness and goodness increase among the people.

KING AŚOKA

Study the teachings of the great sages of all sects impartially.

GAMPOPA

Enlightenment is the only thing of worth in its own right and all other things, be they great or small, can only properly be values in proportion as they contribute to that end or else impede its attainment.

MARCO PALLIS

The pupil must regain the child state it has lost before the first sound can fall upon its ears.

Tibetan Precept

What causes a person to generate the mind of enlightenment? . . . seeing people in this final age being ignorant, shameless, stingy, jealous, full of suffering, vicious, idle and faithless.

K'UEI-CHI

Is it not an illogical attitude on our part to take the sense-world as the starting point of all our ratiocination and to build up our intellectual structure of reality on it? Would it not rather be more logical and sure of results if we try to interpret this world, as experienced by our senses, by the aid of ideas growing out of our inmost perceptions?

D. T. SUZUKI

LIVING THE WAY

Faith is the wealth here best for man—by faith the flood is crossed.

Khuddaka Nikāya

Depend not on words but on the meaning, depend not on knowledge but on wisdom.

Vimalakīrti Sūtra

The wise do not approve of loving-kindness without intelligence, nor do they approve of intelligence without loving-kindness; because one without the other prevents us from reaching the highest path.

Devala

Many do not know that we are here in this world to live in harmony. Those who know this, do not fight against each other.

The Dhammapada

The ultimate aim of Buddhist doctrine and method is to enable us to transcend our humanity, not wallow in it. For sufficient unto our own egotistical self and ignorant of our innate Buddha-nature, we remain trivial and pitiful things, of little more significance in the universal flux than the earthworm, which at least usefully turns over the soil. But once human nature sets out on its spiritual quest . . . which is the only profundity in our ephemerality, it becomes noble, even sublime.

Harold Stewart

Always be a companion to others and not yourself at center. In acting as a support to others lies true equanimity of heart.

Gyōgi

No matter what it is, if we are afraid of losing it, we will lose it but if we are willing to give it up, we will get it.

Tōyo Tenshitsu

But we are not able to practice meditation. When we try, we soon grow confused, being attacked by various delusive thoughts. . . . Our ears seem to be listening to the teaching of Buddhism but, inwardly, we have arrogance and wicked thoughts more tempestuous than the ocean. In our mouths, we speak of the emptiness of things but, in our hearts, egotism towers higher than a mountain.

Shōkū

All beings tremble before danger, all fear death ... life is dear to all. When a man considers this, he does not kill or cause to kill.[*]

The Dhammapada

One who realises that he is in delusion is not greatly deluded, and one who realises that he is in darkness is not in total darkness.

WONHYO

What all schools of the *Mahāyāna* try to do is to live this life of karma and relativity and yet to live, at the same time, a life of transcendence, a life of spiritual freedom, a life not tied down to the chain of causation.... Immanence is conceivable only with transcendence and transcendence with immanence; when the one is made to mean anything without the other, neither becomes intelligible.

D. T. SUZUKI

All beings should be unharmed, self-controlled, calm in mind and gentle.

KING AŚOKA

The mind struggling to defeat
This cloud cover of no substance
Obscures instead
   the light of the moon.

IPPEN

One is powerless to reverse the working out of karma, the accumulated past of mankind, to remove the inevitable circumstances that it determines or to overcome the inherent limitations of finite existence, for these are burdens that we must all bear.

HAROLD STEWART

We know that the revelation of these (Buddhist) mysteries was clearly not the work of man.

The Travels of Fa-hsien

---

[*] "Never to wrong others takes one a long way toward peace of mind. People who know no self-restraint lead stormy and disordered lives, passing their time in a state of fear commensurate with the injuries they do to others, never able to relax." (Seneca)

LIVING THE WAY

The pathetic hope, fostered by the mystique of 'progress', that by a successive accumulation of human contrivances, saṃsāra itself will somehow be, if not abolished, permanently tilted in a comfortable direction is as incompatible with Buddhist realism as with historical probability.

MARCO PALLIS

Amongst those who hate, let us live in love.

The Dhammapada

When all beings are tortured by avarice, passion, ill-humour, infatuation and folly, and are constantly threatened by the misery of birth-and-death, disease and decay, how can the Bodhisattva live among them and not feel pity for them? Of all good virtues, loving-kindness stands foremost. It is the source of all merit. . . . It is the mother of all Buddhas.

DEVALA

It is good not to kill living beings; it is good not only to spend little but to own the minimum of property.

KING AŚOKA

One concentrates one's mind beyond the realm of language and keeps away from meaningless arguments and disturbing thoughts.

K'UEI-CHI

The all-important thing is to have a true heart, whether one's outward appearance is good or bad.

HŌNEN

The affirmative aspect of Buddhism consists in the incessant struggle for the realisation of personality. The cessation of suffering, and the achievement of happiness, is taught as lying in the perfection of personality.

RYUCHI FUJII

At the very beginning (of one's spiritual path), it is indispensably necessary to have the most profound aversion for the interminable sequence of repeated deaths and births.

GAMPOPA

People of the world, parents and children, brothers and sisters, husbands and wives, and other family members and kinsmen, should respect and love each other, refraining from hatred and envy. They should share things with others, and not be greedy and miserly, always speak friendly words with a pleasing smile, and not hurt each other. . . . If one disagrees with others and grows angry, however small one's grudge and enmity may be in this life, these will increase in the life to come until they grow into a mass of hostility.

Sūtra on the Buddha of Immeasurable Life

A sentient being is made whole through experiencing the activity of faith. . . . Faith is the one and only foundation upon which we are enabled to find a purpose greater than our own petty self-interests, a meaning beyond the mere satisfaction of our selfish physiological and psychological drives. It saves us from ego-centrism. It transforms primitive desire into universal desire.

WASUI TATSUGUCHI

Human hindsight, on looking back at worldly failure, loss of family and friends, of health and wealth, of rank and reputation, beholds the wreck or frustration of every hope or desire; and yet in the long view all may have proved salutary, though at times painful, steps in our spiritual growth.

HAROLD STEWART

Overcome anger by peacefulness; overcome evil by good. Overcome the mean by generosity; and the person who lies by truth.

The Dhammapada

An unschooled beggar woman in Tibet, strong in the faith of the Buddha, has a more enviable lot than many an eminent professor in other lands whose obsessive pursuit of purely samsaric investigations constitutes an obstacle a hundred times more insurmountable than mere illiteracy and some degree of petty superstition could ever be for that poor woman. . . . Her simple faith, however limited, must count as an elementary knowledge, whereas colossal erudition directed, not to the centre but to numberless peripheral phenomena, must count as a peculiarly pretentious form of ignorance.

MARCO PALLIS

One who does wrong should be forgiven as far as it is possible to forgive them.

KING AŚOKA

If a man watches not for *Nirvāṇa*, his cravings grow like a creeper and he jumps from death to death like a monkey in the forest, from one tree without fruit to another.

The Dhammapada

The traditional Far Eastern wisdom is to withhold critical condemnation and to accept tentatively and for the time being whatever existence has to offer, just as it is; then to wait in patient detachment to see how it is going to develop; and finally to act in harmony with nature, just as the supple bamboo bends gently in the wind and recovers when it has passed. Such non-action transcends both action and inaction. It acts always without partisan bias and wishful regard to the fruits.

HAROLD STEWART

One must know that misfortune, being the means of leading one to the Doctrine, is also a guru.

GAMPOPA

If we carefully observe the countless varieties of birds and beasts, even tiny insects, we shall discover that they love their children, long to be near their parents, live in couples. . . . How can we not feel pity when pain is inflicted on them or people take their lives? . . . Obviously it is wrong to make others suffer, to torture living creatures or to force even the humblest person to do anything against their will.

KENKŌ

Happiness in this world, and the next, is difficult to obtain without much love for the Dharma, much self-examination, much respect, much fear (of evil), and much enthusiasm.

KING AŚOKA

It is not in the nature of self-power to transcend itself. If it becomes involved in this vain attempt, not knowing its own limitations, the outcome will be the ruination of self.

D. T. SUZUKI

It is said in a sutra: 'The state of enlightenment is not something that is to be acquired by practice or to be created. In the end, it is unobtainable [for it is given from the beginning].'

The Awakening of Faith in the Mahāyāna

A man sometimes learns, for the first time, how mistaken his way of life has been only when he unexpectedly falls ill and is about to depart this world. . . . A man should bear firmly in mind that death is always threatening and never, for an instant, forget it. If he does this, why should the impurities bred in him by this world not grow lighter and his heart not develop an earnest resolve to cultivate the way of the Buddha?

KENKŌ

Buddha proclaimed countless teachings,
Each one revealing the purest truth.
Just as each breeze and every drop of rain
Refreshes the forest,
There is no sutra that does not lead to salvation.
Grasp the essence of each branch
And stop trying to rank the Buddha's teachings.

RYŌKAN

Remember that it is useless to try to force those to believe who will not, for even the Buddha himself cannot do that.

HŌNEN

Victory brings hate, because the defeated man is unhappy. He who surrenders victory and defeat, this man finds joy.

The Dhammapada

Bodhisattvas . . . do not cling to the appearance of permanence in
    things,
Nor do they cling to the appearance of annihilation.

Avataṃsaka Sūtra

Buddhism does not share modern Western man's restless and aggressive attitude of self-assertion, an extroverted optimism scarcely supported by the actual conditions of worldly existence. . . . It adopts neither of the sentimental attitudes of pessimism or optimism.

Instead, the Buddha regards universal existence with detached Wisdom and impartial Compassion. The aim of his teaching and method is liberation from all partial and illusory viewpoints, coloured by desire and aversion, into a state of peace and well-being.

HAROLD STEWART

People see only the good they do saying, 'I have done this worthy deed.' But they do not say, 'I have done this reprehensible deed.' This tendency is difficult to see. One should think like this: 'It is these things that lead to violence, cruelty, anger, pride and jealousy. Let me not ruin myself with them.' And, further, one should think: 'This leads to happiness in this world and the next.'

KING AŚOKA

To have but few desires and be satisfied with simple things is the sign of a superior person.

GAMPOPA

The law of karma, the miseries of worldly existence . . . the certainty of death and the uncertainty of the time of death. Weigh these things in your minds, and devote yourself to the study and practice of Remembrance.

MILAREPA

Till the great leap in the dark is taken, faith in the Buddha's enlightenment must be our lamp, since all that stems from light is light, and even our darkness, did we but know it, is none other than the dazzlement inflicted by a radiance too intense for samsaric eyes to bear.

MARCO PALLIS

It may be said that there is the principle of Suchness and that it can permeate into ignorance. Through the force of this permeation, Suchness causes the deluded mind to loathe the suffering of birth-and-death and to aspire for *Nirvāṇa*. Because this mind, though still deluded, is now possessed with loathing and aspiration, it permeates into Suchness in that it induces Suchness to manifest itself. Thus a person comes to believe in their essential nature.

The Awakening of Faith in the Mahāyāna

All people are my children. What I desire for my own children, and I desire their welfare and happiness both in this world and the next, that I desire for all. You do not understand to what extent I desire this, and if some of you do understand, you do not understand the full extent of my desire.

KING AŚOKA

As the bee takes the essence of the flower and flies away without destroying its beauty and perfume, so let the sage wander in this life.

The Dhammapada

Even though there is a touch of good intention, it is like writing on water; waves of greed and anger are too high, and no traces of goodness are left.

SHŌKŪ

There is not one shred of historical evidence to substantiate the fiction that any society staffed by men is perfectible. All that we know of the past goes to prove the world's chronic corruptibility, at least so long as it is under human management. Its defects seem inbuilt by design, to prevent our permanent attachment to any of its forms of impermanence.

HAROLD STEWART

Though it is regrettable not to have met Shakyamuni* Buddha during his lifetime, nevertheless it is the greatest of blessings to be born into this world and have a chance to listen to his profound teachings. The likelihood of this happening can be compared to that of a blind turtle placing its head through a hole in a piece of drift-wood upon emerging from the ocean.

HŌNEN

Obscuring passions, being the means of reminding one of Divine Wisdom (which gives deliverance from them) are not to be avoided (if rightly used . . . to reach disillusionment).

GAMPOPA

---

* 'Sage of the Shakya clan'; the historical Buddha, also known as Gautama, who was born into the Shakya royal family in Lumbinī (present-day Nepal).

LIVING THE WAY

If we are not enlightened or saved originally, there is no possibility of us attaining enlightenment or salvation at all.

YOSHITO HAKEDA

The Buddhas and Bodhisattvas desire to liberate all men, spontaneously permeating them [with their spiritual influences] and never forsaking them. Through the power of the wisdom that is one [with Suchness], they manifest activities in response [to the needs of men] as they see and hear them.

The Awakening of Faith in the Mahāyāna

If the senses are purified by detachment from desire and no longer crave and cling to worldly pleasures that pollute their innocent clarity, then sensuous forms can become the exponents of that which transcends the senses and so can lead to a realisation of *Śūnyatā*, the Formless, that is the background of all forms. If *saṃsāra* is contemplated with such perfectly tranquil detachment, it can reveal—even in this life—a fore-glimpse, however brief, of the bliss of *Nirvāṇa*.

HAROLD STEWART

For hate is not conquered by hate; hate is conquered by love. This is the law eternal.

The Dhammapada

Contact (between religions) is good. One should listen to and respect the doctrines professed by others.... All should be well-learned in the good doctrines of other religions.

KING AŚOKA

The attainer of enlightenment is not 'this person so-and-so' but rather it is by the ending of the dream of one's 'so-and-so-ness' that enlightenment arises.... When all things have become transparent to the point of allowing the Uncreated Light to shine through them, there is nothing further to become.

MARCO PALLIS

As soon as we realise our weakness in doing good, real goodness is performed.

SHŌKŪ

It is less defiant than foolhardy to boast that transience does not make one long to leave this world, since ceaseless change has the final say, removing not only all one's pleasures and occupations but, at last, life itself without asking one's permission or preference of time or place. But notice that it is attachment to life, not life itself, from which we must escape. Buddhists are enjoined to live out their still-unexhausted karma with detachment, not merely to evade it. . . . For when the latent causes of the past have matured and current conditions are favourable and ready, the karmic fruit cannot help but ripen and fall.

HAROLD STEWART

Those that would make an end of sorrow and come to the bound of happiness must establish firmly the root of Faith and immovably set their thoughts upon Enlightenment.

SHANTIDEVA

A Bodhisattva who is in fear of mortal existence should rely upon the power of . . . the *Tathāgata*.

Vimalakīrti Sūtra

Such considerations as these move me to wonder what sort of past actions provide the conditions necessary for birth in human form. What did I do to cause it? I am not sure. In any case, it is very difficult to gain the Dharma, but now we have it. What a waste it would be then to live vainly, without giving heed to the teachings or putting them into practice. To die without making the least spiritual progress; how shameful!

HŌNEN

The essential nature of all Bodhisattvas is a great loving heart and all sentient beings constitute the object of its love. . . . In order to emancipate them, Bodhisattvas are inspired with great spiritual energy and mingle themselves in the filth of birth-and-death.

NĀGĀRJUNA

However valiantly you have wakened the aspiration for enlightenment, take your active practice down a peg or two. Give your heart the higher place, practice the lower.

KYŌRENJA

LIVING THE WAY

The whole world is tormented by words
And there is no one who does without words.
But only in so far as one is free from words,
Does one really understand words.

SARAHA

Those who know that this body is like the foam of a wave, the shadow
of a mirage . . . will never see the king of death.

The Dhammapada

Buddhism teaches neither a cast-iron determinism nor an arbitrary
predestination: man does possess free will, but this is so conditioned
by past actions and present circumstances, both individual and col-
lective, that he can only to an increasingly limited degree rearrange
finite things and events, and modify their future appearances nearer
to his desires. At the beginning of a game of chess, the hopeful player
has a choice of a large number of possible moves; in the end, no matter what move the defeated player makes, he puts his king in check.

HAROLD STEWART

Wakening aspiration for enlightenment is best accomplished by
stealth.

HŌNEN

If the self is only a mechanical succession of various mental activities,
how is it possible to recognise such a changing succession of phenomena? The absolute negation of self contradicts its own claim. This
negation presupposes the existence of the negating self. Therefore,
self-negation means the affirmation of self in some form or other. To
make knowledge possible, there must be a unifying consciousness
which constructs our experience. Such a conscious self must remain
identical throughout our various changing experiences. The conscious self must transcend experience, otherwise it cannot make
experience possible.

RYUCHI FUJII

Take the lowest place and you shall reach the highest.

MILAREPA

Those who are only capable of feeling their own selfish sufferings may enter into *Nirvāṇa* [and not trouble themselves with the sufferings of other creatures like themselves]; but the Bodhisattva who feels in himself all the sufferings of his fellow-beings as his own, how can he bear the thought of leaving others behind while he is on his way to final emancipation? *Nirvāṇa* in truth consists in rejoicing at others being made happy.... He who feels a universal love for his fellow-creatures will rejoice in distributing blessings among them and find his *Nirvāṇa* in so doing.

DEVALA

The Bodhisattva loves all sentient beings as his own children. When they are sick, he is sick too. When they are recovered, he is well again.... This [sympathetic] illness of the Bodhisattva comes from his all-embracing love.

Vimalakīrti Sūtra

Moralism, as the conscious effort by the individual or social will to be good or do good, is foredoomed to failure because, no matter how cleverly disguised by mankind's talent for personal deception or public hypocrisy, it is really motivated by the vested interests of the self and inadvertently betrays a lack of faith in any power higher than the human. Such attempts at self-help are at best palliatives, not remedies: they may prove partially efficacious, temporarily relieving our sufferings, but they never provide a complete and permanent cure.

HAROLD STEWART

Long accustomed to contemplating Love and Pity
I have forgotten all difference between myself and others.

MILAREPA

Rather than trying to perform good acts, just stop doing evil.

MYŌZEN

The Thought of Enlightenment has arisen within me I know not how, even as a gem might be gotten by a blind man from a dunghill; it is an elixir made to destroy death in the world, an unfailing treasure to relieve the world's poverty, a supreme balm to allay the world's sickness, a tree under which may rest all creatures wearied with wandering over life's paths, a bridge open to all wayfarers for passing over hard ways, a moon of thought arising to cool the fever of the world's sin, a great sun driving away the gloom of the world's ignorance, a fresh butter created by the churning of the milk of the Dharma. For the caravan of beings . . . hungering to taste of happiness, this banquet of bliss is prepared that will satisfy all creatures coming to it.

SHANTIDEVA

Do not denounce the teachings followed by others.
With wholeness of heart give rise to compassion;
Do not be forgetful of others' sorrow. . . .
With wholeness of heart
Disclose a gentle countenance;
Do not manifest marks of anger and intolerance.
With wholeness of heart
Dwell firmly in humility's insights;
Do not arouse a spirit of arrogance.
With wholeness of heart
Discern the sources of impurity;
Do not generate a mind that cherishes attachments.
With wholeness of heart
Contemplate the reality of impermanence;
Do not awaken thoughts of greed and desire. . . .
With wholeness of heart
Rectify your own faults;
Do not revile others for their transgressions.
With wholeness of heart
Sport in the activity of transforming others. . . .
Do not indulge in unwholesome acts.
With wholeness of heart
Aspire for the Land of Peace.

IPPEN

The *Tathāgata* dispels forever
The doubts of sentient beings,
And all the aspirations of their hearts
He brings to complete fulfillment.

Avataṃsaka Sūtra

Because there is great pleasure it is called great *Nirvāṇa*. *Nirvāṇa* is without pleasure and, because it possesses the four aspects of pleasure, it is called great *Nirvāṇa*. What are these four? The first is eradication of all pleasures. If pleasures are not eradicated, it is called pain. If there is pain, it cannot be called great pleasure. Because one eradicates pleasure, there is no pain. Being without pain and without pleasure is great pleasure. The nature of *Nirvāṇa* is absence of pain and absence of pleasure. Hence, it is called great pleasure. With this meaning, it is called great *Nirvāṇa*.

Nirvāṇa Sūtra

Most likely, you will never awaken any genuine compassion; but you must harbour hatred of no one.

Ichigon Hōdan

The *Mahāyāna* has long recognised the close affinity between sexual passion and rage. Violent outbursts of lust and anger, the frantic ravings of the imprisoned splendour to be let out of its corporeal cage, are warning signs that our religious aspirations are suppressed and unsatisfied. We feel irritable and annoyed because we are compelled to expend most of our precious life and time in pursuit of mundane and transitory objectives when, in our hearts, we know that they should be devoted wholly to the search for Liberation and Enlightenment. . . . Having abandoned the spiritual quest and settled for material comfort and contentment, 'most men,' as Thoreau observed, 'lead lives of quiet desperation.'

HAROLD STEWART

'Wherever the Buddha comes to stay, there is no state, town or village that is not blessed by his virtues. The whole country reposes in peace and harmony. The sun and the moon shine with pure brilliance; winds rise and rains fall at the right time. There is no calamity or epidemic and so the country becomes wealthy, and its people enjoy peace. Soldiers and weapons become useless; and people esteem virtue, practice benevolence and diligently cultivate courteous modesty.' . . . The Buddha continued, 'But after I have departed from this world, my teaching will gradually decline and people will fall prey to flattery and deceit, and commit various evils.'

Sūtra on the Buddha of Immeasurable Life

Upon introspection, I realise that I have not observed a single Buddhist precept or succeeded in the practice of meditation. . . . In addition, the mind of the common man is easily distracted by conditions around it . . . it is confused, vacillating and unable to concentrate. . . . Without the sword of undefiled wisdom, how will we extricate ourselves from the fetters of karma and harmful passions? Unable to sever these fetters, how will we deliver ourselves from the bondage of the transmigration of birth-and-death in order to realise emancipation? This is indeed lamentable and disheartening.

HŌNEN

You should resolutely do worthy deeds with decorum, strive to do more good, control and purify yourselves, wash off the mind's defilements, be sincere in word and deed, and allow no contradiction between what you think and what you do. Seek your own emancipation and then turn to saving others.

Sūtra on the Buddha of Immeasurable Life

Our secular education has for so long instilled into us the fallacy of materialism, that we now take as axiomatic the metaphysically false premise that this world of matter is alone real and that this life is the only state of existence that we shall ever know. . . . But from our first awareness of pain on being born into this world until we resign our waking consciousness at death, the basic and incontrovertible fact, known before all else, is our human consciousness.

HAROLD STEWART

During the first five hundred years after the Buddha's passing into *Nirvāṇa*, my disciples will be steadfast in learning wisdom. During the second five hundred years, they will be steadfast in learning meditation. During the third five hundred years, they will be steadfast in learning much teaching and chanting sutras. During the fourth five hundred years, they will be steadfast in constructing pagodas and temples, and performing meritorious acts and repentances. During the fifth five hundred years, the pure Dharma will be hidden and there will be much conflict and debate. . . . This is now the last dharma-age . . . [and] out of billions of sentient beings who will seek to perform practices and cultivate the Way . . . not one will gain realisation.... This one gate—the Pure Land way—is the only path that affords passage.

Sūtra of the Great Assembly

With all the virtues and roots of good that Bodhisattvas have accumulated, they do not seek the sustained bliss for their own sake, but think only of freeing all sentient beings from pain; hence, they aspire to grasp all sentient beings and to bring them all together to birth in the Buddha's realm of happiness.

T'AN-LUAN

It is like the urgent desire one feels when swept up in a passionate relationship in this world of swiftly-changing colours; so too would one passionately give anything, even one's life, when one encounters the Buddhist teaching.

HŌNEN

One who has acquired a gem that prevents drowning—the mind aspiring for enlightenment—enters the ocean of birth-and-death but does not sink or succumb. As a diamond may be immersed in water for one hundred thousand aeons without destruction or alteration, so is the mind aspiring for enlightenment, which may be submerged in all the karma of blind passions in birth-and-death for endless aeons, and yet not be damaged or destroyed.

GENSHIN

Trust is the initial gate for entering the Dharma.... It is for this reason that the sutras and treatises state: 'Unlike a person with hands who can reach out to a place of rare jewels and grab them as they wish, one without hands is unable to obtain anything. Trusting [in the Dharma] is like this.'

HUI-YÜAN

'Blind passions' refer to pains that torment the body and afflictions which distress the heart and mind.

SHINRAN

Even though a person lacks knowledge and broad learning, why should they not possess the capacity to trust?

SEIKAKU

LIVING THE WAY

The three treasures, which are Buddha, the Buddhist Law and the Buddhist Community, should be given sincere reverence, for they are the final refuge of all living things. Few people are so bad that they cannot be taught their truth.

Prince Shōtoku

When I (Buddha) look at living beings
I see them drowning in a sea of suffering;
Therefore I do not show myself,
Causing them to thirst for me.
Then, when their minds are filled with yearning,
At last do I appear and preach the Dharma to them.

Lotus Sūtra

There is no land where the moonlight does not reach,
Finding a place in the hearts of those who would abide in its light.

Hōnen

'This mind attains Buddhahood' means that the mind becomes Buddha; 'This mind is itself Buddha' means that there is no Buddha apart from the mind. This is like the relationship of fire and wood: fire arises from wood; it cannot exist apart from the wood. Because it cannot exist apart from the wood, it consumes the wood. The wood, on the other hand, is consumed by the fire; it becomes the fire.

T'an-luan

Paradoxical as it may seem, on plunging down into that chaos of negation, in which the conscious ego fears that it will suffer dissolution and deprivation of its individuality in a black non-existence, instead an instantaneous miracle occurs. One's real identity is discovered at the very moment in which the ego is extinguished in nothingness. Out of that dark abyss of absence and annihilation rises one's true personality; one's being is infinitely expanded and enhanced ... in a supra-individual and oceanic brightness, both positive and plenary, as one soars into the Void of Infinite Light. These two inseparable phases in one's spiritual awakening occur in a single timeless instant.

Harold Stewart

The 'Buddhism of Faith' is in the direct line of Buddhist orthodoxy. Surrender in faith involves a high degree of extinction of separate self-hood, partly because one does not rely on oneself, or one's own power, partly because one sees the futility of all conscious personal efforts and allows oneself to be 'carried' to salvation, and partly because one does not claim any special privileges as due to superior merit or wisdom.

Pride has always been a sin to which the more advanced Buddhists were particularly prone. Now they are taught humbly to accept gifts from another, whom they can only perceive in faith. All pride in our intellect and the purity of our heart sets up a self against others. If the intellect is seen as futile, the heart as corrupt, that self is deflated. The grace of the Absolute alone can carry us across and our own personal schemes and endeavours are quite trivial. For it must never be forgotten that that which is represented to the relatively ignorant, in the form of a personal saviour and a paradise, is exactly the same thing which is taught to the relatively learned as the Absolute itself.

Following out the logic of Buddhist dialectics, perfection is found only in its extinction, and it is manifested only where it becomes quite indiscernible. . . . A sincere heart and belief, unaware of the merit of its sincerity, is all that is needed. The Buddha's demand that, in order to be saved, one should learn to do nothing in particular, is fulfilled in this way as perfectly as in any other.

EDWARD CONZE

CHAPTER FOUR

IMMEASURABLE LIFE

—*Amida Buddha and the Pure Land*

Introduction

The following chapter is devoted to the largest tradition of Buddhism in East Asia and the one that has been, by far, the most influential among lay people. It is also the last great development in its history, beyond which it had no further to go. In this sense, it represents a consummation of everything that came before it.

The fundamental purpose of Pure Land Buddhism is to provide a vehicle for the spiritual needs of ordinary people who are not capable of special attainments and who find themselves burdened by the limitations and problems imposed by everyday life. It addresses itself directly to the person who is unable to do anything to fulfill the traditional requirements of practice imposed by the older Buddhist schools which are largely geared towards the observation of austerities, meditation and other requirements that are more easily pursued in a monastic context. It is the only Buddhist path for flawed, troubled and confused people who, doubtlessly, represent the great majority of humanity today.

So what is it that makes this path so accessible and how does it justify abrogating what are often considered the normal expectations of Buddhist practice? Firstly, it conveys the traditional teachings concerning reality through tangible forms that are attractive, compelling, intelligible and in conformity with the actual capacities of people in the world. This, precisely, is what has accounted for its great and enduring popularity for many centuries.

As we have seen earlier in this work, the highest reality in Buddhism is often depicted in negative terms. That is to say, we read that it is formless, intangible, empty and beyond words. However, it is very difficult—impossible for most in fact—to come to terms with this way of viewing it even if, intellectually, we may understand why such a reality needs to possess attributes largely based on negation. Nevertheless, Buddhism teaches that there is not only a 'wisdom' dimension at the heart of all things but also one of 'compassion.' The latter aspect has vital implications for how it becomes disclosed to us.

The passages we encountered earlier in this work did not just focus on the ineffable and transcendent features of this reality. They also tell us that it is the highest good, complete happiness and supreme enlightenment. As it is also intelligent, such a positive spiritual force must seek to reach out to those who are not enlightened, in a way that its blessings can readily be made known. This is its compassionate response to the needs of our benighted condition, full of affliction, contradictions and tribulation.

Therefore, what we find in the Pure Land sutras is a portrayal of ultimate reality clothed in forms that express its compassion in the most direct and vivid manner. We are told about Amida, Buddha of Infinite Light (*Amitābha*) and Immeasurable Life (*Amitāyus*), who makes a 'Primal Vow' to take, to his Pure Land adorned with the utmost bliss (*Sukhāvatī*), anyone who calls his Name. We also read about the extraordinary features of that realm (for example, trees made of jewels, ponds filled with gem stones and wondrous light-emitting lotuses, celestial music constantly playing, beautiful flowers descending from the sky, and birds communicating the Buddha's teachings in melodious song). Some are taken aback by these accounts, which strike them as merely poetic and difficult to accept as anything other than stories concocted by enthusiastic writers simply projecting their own spiritual fantasies.

This might seem an understandable response, at first glance, but it fails to comprehend the deeper significance of these descriptions. Given the prominence of compassion in Pure Land Buddhism, especially in light of the degraded state of humanity in the present age, it is paramount that it be conveyed to ordinary people in a way that is easily understood and made compelling for them. Therefore, this compassion takes the initiative towards us making itself known in the form of Amida Buddha and the Pure Land—it is the highest and most exalted level of personification that the ultimate reality, or Dharma-Body, can assume. Seeing as it has had to adopt an appearance in order to communicate what it is, 'Light' and 'Life' are the most perfect expressions of what Amida represents, whose name means 'Infinite.' Considered in this way, Amida is perfectly real in the sense that the presence, wisdom and compassion inherent in Enlightenment itself are also very real and, therefore, capable of being known and experienced by us in this life.

These compassionate manifestations, therefore, are none other than those adopted by the Eternal Buddha in order to reveal true reality to the people of our world. They received embodiment through individuals, over time, who became awakened to this reality and committed their insights to the texts that have come down to us in the form of the Pure Land sutras.

And so it is with the notion of the Pure Land itself. If we had to use everyday language to capture the sense of inconceivable bliss and liberation of *Nirvāṇa*, what we find in the sutras is certainly a most beautiful and effective means of doing so and in a way that meets the pressing spiritual needs of ordinary people. While these narratives might seem highly fanciful, we must remember not to become overly captivated by the exotic depictions of spiritual reality that we find in the sutras seeing as they are only forms—albeit very powerful ones capable of attracting our deepest aspiration for a realm of beauty and blessedness which, in any case, completely surpasses our ability to comprehend conceptually.

What lies behind such forms is much greater—even more wonderful—than what is stated. These texts constitute a sacred veil. We can either just admire the 'fabric' of these richly imaginative evocations from the outside, beautiful as they are, or we can ever so tentatively lift this veil to catch a glimpse of the formless light of the Dharma-Body which sustains all these compassionate disclosures. In a way, of course, these texts constitute symbols but not in the sense of being empty signs pointing back to us as their human fabricators but as intimating something inconceivable which we can never fully grasp, in this life at least, except through these images of joy and wonder.

The other feature of Pure Land Buddhism that challenges some people is the emphasis on what is often referred to as 'faith'—a word which, unfortunately, has fallen on hard times. When understood in its fullest significance, it denotes, as perhaps no other English word can do, a range of profound and complex attitudes which are perfectly Buddhist. Shinran describes it as an entrusting mind 'full of truth, reality and sincerity; the mind of ultimacy, accomplishment, reliance and reverence; the mind of discernment, distinctness, clarity and faithfulness; the mind of aspiration and exultation; the mind of delight, joy, gladness and happiness; hence, it is completely untainted by the hindrance of doubt.' The term that he used to capture this 'entrusting mind' is *shinjin* (or *citta-prasāda* in Sanskrit) which means 'true and clear heart and mind' because it represents the mind of the Buddha to which we become awakened. This is a far cry from any notion of faith as resembling blind belief. In essence, *shinjin* is wisdom (*prajñā*). It is a form of direct spiritual knowledge ('the eye of the heart') that sees things as they are because it is a vision imparted to us by Amida Buddha, even though we remain 'foolish beings' captive to our myriad desires and delusions.

The realisation of *shinjin*, as the breaking through of the Buddha's beneficent karmic force (also known as 'Other-Power') is what tempers our 'blind passions' here and now and quells them at the time of death when we attain 'birth in the Pure Land' (that is, realise *Nirvāṇa*). The way in which the awakening of *shinjin* is manifested is through the *nembutsu*—the mindful invocation of Amida's Name in the form of *Namu Amida Butsu* ('I take refuge in Amida Buddha'). When uttered with a heart of faith, the sound of the *nembutsu* heralds the working of Amida who comes forth, on our lips, as a living presence. This is both our call to the Buddha and the compassionate call we receive in response. When we 'hear' the Name for the first time, and understand its significance, we are then led naturally to say the *nembutsu* in gratitude while fully recognising that every genuine utterance is permeated by the 'true heart and mind' of Amida Buddha.

Even those for whom *shinjin* does not feel certain or settled, great benefit can still be derived from simply saying the *nembutsu*—not because it is some kind of 'magical' phrase but because the very act of reaching out to Amida through his Name, even if it is unsure and faltering at first, signifies an aspiration and a seeking of refuge which, in time, will elicit a definitive response whereby we come to feel 'constantly illumined by the light of that Buddha's heart, grasped and protected, never to be abandoned' (Shan-tao).

IMMEASURABLE LIFE

Life in the human world is but momentary and ephemeral; life in the Pure Land is the eternal, blissful fruit. . . . You will be born in the land of bliss only through having the entrusting heart—a single-minded and unwavering reliance on the *Tathāgata* without any calculations.

RENNYO

That Pure Land, from whose blessedness we shall never fall.

HŌNEN

Faith is the heart and mind without doubt; it is *shinjin*, which is true and real. It is the heart and mind free of that which is empty and transitory.*

SHINRAN

When sentient beings prostrate themselves to the Buddha, the Buddha sees them. When people call to him, he hears them. When they think about him, he thinks about them. In this way, the deeds, words and thoughts—the three kinds of action of Amida Buddha and his devotees—become one in the intimacy of parent and children. For this reason, it is called an 'intimate relation.'

SHAN-TAO

Amida, according to the teaching of Shin, has no intention of interfering with the working of karma, for it has to run its course in this world; the debt incurred by one person is to be paid by them and not by another. . . . As long as Amida takes care of you and karma has its own course to follow, what use is there in making petitions to any higher powers?

D. T. SUZUKI

---

* "Dharma-body as Suchness always fills the minds of all sentient beings and when beings realise *shinjin* . . . for the first time this becomes known to them. Before the realisation of *shinjin*, they are unaware of it, for the unenlightened, delusional minds of beings and the Dharma-Body as Suchness that fills them stand in absolute opposition and mutual negation. For this reason, the basic *Mahāyāna* teaching that all beings possess Buddha-nature is not a form of pantheism. Through the transformation that occurs with the realisation of *shinjin*, this opposition is overcome, and the unenlightened mind becomes aware of the Dharma-Body or true reality that fills it. Thus, to realise *shinjin* is to return to one's fundamental reality." (Yoshifumi Ueda and Dennis Hirota, *Shinran: An Introduction to His Thought*, pp. 175–76)

You should not have the slightest doubt that sentient beings who seriously rely on Amida Buddha, for resolving the matter of the greatest importance of the afterlife, will all be saved.

RENNYO

Regarding the capacity of ordinary people of this age of declining Dharma to attain birth into the Land of Ultimate Bliss, do not doubt it even though your religious practice may seem insufficient.... Do not allow doubts to hinder you for, as we are told, Amida does not discriminate among beings on account of their behaviour.... There may not be one of us who is capable of right living. Indeed, we commit misdeeds incessantly. Nevertheless, we do not doubt the possibility of attaining birth. Has not Shakyamuni testified that he himself was, at one time, full of defiling passions?

HŌNEN

The experience of faith in Amida Buddha is a consummation in terms of a well-integrated personality that is fully aware of the mortal and spiritual within us.

WASUI TATSUGUCHI

Although my defiled life is filled with all kinds of desires and delusions, my mind is playing in the Pure Land.

SHINRAN

Whoever recites the name of *Amitābha** Buddha, whether in the present time, or in future time, will surely see the Buddha and never become separated from him. By reason of that association, just as one who mingles with a perfume maker becomes permeated with the same perfumes, so they will be perfumed by *Amitābha*'s compassion and become enlightened without any other expedient means.

Śūraṅgama Sūtra

Amida's will to help us out of the ocean of birth-and-death is none other than our faith in Amida. In Amida, faith is the will to help and, in us, this will becomes faith; his will and our faith are consubstantial as it were, hence a perfect correspondence between the two.

D.T. SUZUKI

* 'Infinite Light' in Sanskrit.

IMMEASURABLE LIFE

People who take up scholarly study—though they may have long yearned for the world beyond—usually lose their aspiration.

KYŌRENJA

The person of *shinjin* is nothing but the manifestation of Amida's working.

YOSHIFUMI UEDA

Seeking the world beyond is no different from carrying out your life on the paths of this world. This day is already at dusk. How easy it is to be slack in your labour. The year, too, drifts to a close; a lifetime is elapsing without any sense of urgency. At night, lie down and lament this meaningless procession of hours and, at dawn, awaken and resolve to endeavour in your practice to the day's end. When slovenly and negligent, set your mind on the transience of samsaric existence. When wayward thoughts take hold in your heart, raise your voice and utter the *nembutsu*.

Ichigon Hōdan

The life of Shin faith has been likened to the relationship between steel and bellows. The steel is cold and hard but, once it is subjected to the bellows, it emanates brightness and heat. It immediately becomes cold and hard again when taken away from the bellows and placed in water. In Shin faith, steel represents us and the bellows symbolise true compassion. As long as we are in touch with true compassion, the instinctive ego, which was once cold and hard, emanates warmth, tenderness and light. But once we forget true compassion, this ego once again becomes cold and hard to create negative karma and consequent hardships for us.

GYODO HAGURI

We often talk about the natures of things. For example, the heat of flames rises towards the sky; water seeks its own level; some kinds of fruit are sour, others are sweet. It is just in the nature of certain kinds of things to have particular qualities. There is not the slightest doubt that we are referring to the same kind of natural process whenever we speak of the Buddha's Primal Vow—the commitment he made to come and meet, when they die, all those who did nothing more than sincerely call out his name, and to guide them to the Pure Land of perfect bliss. This is beyond doubt.

HŌNEN

At last we have now been brought face to face with Amida and his Primal Vow and are like those longing to cross a stream who have found a ferry. As, however, we reflect upon the passing of the days and nights, and how quickly we are drawing near to the realm of shadows, we must make haste and seek deliverance with all our hearts and, forsaking everything else, earnestly lift up our voices and invoke the sacred name; otherwise, our golden opportunity will have passed and nothing be left to us but remorse.

Yōkan

The stress laid on 'Other-Power' provides a salutary counterblast to any form of self-esteem, a fact which makes its teachings peculiarly apt in our own time when deification of the human animal as confined to this world, and a wholescale pandering to its ever-expanding appetites, is being preached on every side. . . . It is in intelligent humility that a truly human greatness is to be found.

Marco Pallis

The human world is one of uncertainty, while the land of bliss is a realm of eternity.

Rennyo

Amida's Primal Vow says nothing about whether we are good or bad, nor does it consider whether our religious practices are many or few. It makes no discrimination between the pure and the impure, and takes no account of time, space, or any other diverse circumstances in our lives. It matters not how we die.

Hōnen

When we were *jiriki* (self-power) believers, we had to run after the Buddha asking him to save us; but when we follow *tariki* (Other-Power), we realise that Amida has been running after us all the time. Only because we did not know this, have we had to transmigrate.

Shōkū

If we are but born in the Pure Land by embarking on Amida's Primal Vow, then none of our cherished desires remain unfulfilled.

Hōnen

IMMEASURABLE LIFE

The medicine is the 'Calling of the Name of Amida Buddha.'... For this medicine, no capital or special wisdom is needed. All one has to do is recite the words with your mouth.... Here indeed is a pivot of fundamental power. Do I hear you say 'Too easy'? 'Such wares are intended only to deceive old men and women.' Many doubt its efficacy and ask of the wise if there is not some other way more suited for clever people. And Shakyamuni pointed straight back at the heart of man and said that within it is to be found the true Buddha-nature.

HAKUIN

The one thing learning has taught me is its utter powerlessness to bring me birth into the Pure Land.

HŌNEN

Beholding the power of the Buddha's Primal Vow, I see that no one who encounters it passes by in vain. It can quickly bring to fullness and perfection the great treasure ocean of virtues.

VASUBANDHU

The virtuous masters of old were superbly accomplished in wisdom and their various forms of practice, and deaths, were splendid as they freely fulfilled their hearts' desire. Most teachers of the different schools at present, though they study texts, possess little resolution to achieve enlightenment. They use the Buddha's words as a bridge for making their way in the world, and turn the sacred teachings into means for supporting their material existence. Thus, their training is wholly for the sake of esteem and profit, and while they idly debate ... days and months pass swiftly by. Suddenly they find that the time of death is upon them and know not what to do.... It is like rushing to dig a well when caught in a drought. From ordinary times, then, set your thoughts wholly on the means by which to resolve the one great matter: breaking free from samsaric existence.

MYŌHEN

We should simply ... give up the inclination to perform various practices and miscellaneous acts, and deeply entrust ourselves to Amida with singleness of thought and wholehearted assurance of our emancipation in the afterlife.

RENNYO

For those of us who are born into this transient world, the Pure Land path is just to wish to leave it and be born into the Land of Bliss. One's birth into that land, in accordance with the intent of Amida Buddha's great vow, is not determined by one's good or bad deeds but, in actuality, depends solely on whether or not one relies on the Buddha's compassion. . . . The path of sages can be compared to the act of travelling toward one's destination over perilous mountain roads, while the Pure Land path is like taking a boat over calm seas. People who have weak legs and poor eyesight are not likely to make it through the mountains. By boat, however, they can get to where they want to go. For such people, it is really the only way they can reach their destination.

Hōnen

The diamond-like mind is true and real *shinjin*. True and real *shinjin* is unfailingly accompanied by [saying] the Name.

Shinran

Make the Pure Land path more important than any other factor in your life, and then the defilement of ignorance cannot harm you. Though you are deluded, this is no obstacle to liberation so long as you value birth in the Pure Land above all else.

Hōnen

Those who aspire for the world beyond cease to do the things they want; for all that they desire in their hearts to do is wrong.

Ichigon Hōdan

From the first, we must acknowledge that we are human beings and, as such, have very limited capacity for wholesome moral action. Only when we have accepted this fact can we rely completely on the Primal Vow of the Buddha. . . . Even though we are afflicted by blind passions and are ignorant worldlings who commit unskillful deeds, all we have to do is call the name of Amida Buddha once, with full confidence in his Vow, and we shall certainly be born in the Pure Land.

Hōnen

The boundless compassion of Amida, when we awaken to it and accept it, melts away to tenderness our deep-seated obstinacy and self-complacency. We are thus enabled to confront every problem open-mindedly, flexibly and without prejudice.

DAIEI KANEKO

An infant turns to its mother without any idea why. There is simply an utter reliance. Entrusting yourself to the Name is like this.

KENSHŌ

Ren-amidabutsu had a dream in which the Deity of the Hachiman shrine declared: 'Birth into the Pure Land does not depend on saying the *nembutsu* once; it does not depend on saying it many times. It depends on the heart.'

Ichigon Hōdan

Simply dedicate yourself to saying the *nembutsu*. This may seem but a pouring of water onto stone, but utter it, and there will be benefit.

MYŌZEN

It is not easy to relax and let go, and plunge into the flood with only a simple phrase as your life-belt and the very nature of things-as-they-are. It is not easy but it is a great relief when you do so.

MARIE BYLES

If you abide in an attitude of self-power, even saying the Name but a single time will be an expression of self-attachment. If you entrust yourself to Other-Power, utterance after utterance ... will be the manifestation of Other-Power.

HŌNEN

The Buddha's mercy is providential but does not, for this very reason, suspend the law of karma. If beings will persist in ignoring that law while coveting the things mercy might have granted them, that mercy itself will reach them in the guise of severity; severity is merciful when this is the only means of provoking a radical *metanoia* (change of out-look), failing which wandering in *saṃsāra* must needs continue indefinitely. The *nembutsu* is our ever-present reminder of this truth; if, in reliance on the Vow, we abandon all wish to attribute victory to ourselves, the unfed ego will surely waste away, leaving us in peace.

MARCO PALLIS

After his attainment of birth in the Pure Land, Hōnen appeared to Jūshin-bō of Miidera in a dream and answered his question: 'Though you ask, Amida Buddha is completely without appearances. One can only say the Name.'

Ichigon Hōdan

In short, without attaching undue importance to the affairs of daily life, just sincerely endeavour to practice the path of *nembutsu* alone. We call this intention the 'heart of truth.'

HŌNEN

Learning may seem important but it is not really necessary. In fact, although you may clarify one doubtful issue through study, in the process you will stumble on other questions and so spend a lifetime resolving doubts, without a chance to utter the *nembutsu* in the peace of your heart. Learning, rather than being an aid to *nembutsu*, is a formidable obstruction.

JŌGAN

In the course of life in this world, the unenlightened person will inevitably feel desire for esteem and wealth. The understanding and practice for birth into the Pure Land, however, must be wholly genuine and real.

SHŌKŌ

Words of the Dharma, for the person aspiring to the world beyond, will not exceed a single page.

KYŌBUTSU

Someone asked Myōhen, 'Is study beneficial when its sole aim is attainment of the world beyond?' He answered, 'At first, your thoughts may be on the world beyond but, later, they will come to be entirely for esteem and possessions.'

Ichigon Hōdan

Dwelling in this world and consciously experiencing its sorrow is an opportunity to weary [of samsaric existence]. Be glad, therefore, at having been born a human being. However shallow our trust, the Primal Vow itself is fathomless; if we simply entrust ourselves to it, then, we will unfailingly attain birth. . . . Vast are the virtues of the Primal

Vow, so rejoice at having encountered it. . . . The *nembutsu* emerging to utterance from our delusional thoughts is like a lotus blossom unstained by the mud. Do not doubt, therefore, that your attainment of birth is settled.

GENSHIN

When I reflect on having met with the effective cause of birth, Other-Power, I realise that it is with this life that I must gain liberation from birth-and-death. Though we encounter Other-Power, we will certainly fall to lower realms again if we idly pass it by to no purpose. Whether or not we part from samsaric existence, then, depends on the present.

MYŌZEN

People who have seriously embraced the aspiration for birth in the Pure Land always have about them a slightly cynical distrust of the world.

HŌNEN

Someone asked Kyūjitsu-bō, 'I say the Name knowing this utterance to be the key to attaining birth in the Pure Land, but my thoughts wander off to the moors and mountains of this world and I say it merely with my lips. What should I do?' He answered, 'When you set out with the idea of coming here, surely you did not think "I'm going there, I'm going there" with every step. You made your way here with your mind full of unrelated thoughts. Nevertheless, you did not cease walking and you have arrived. In this way, once you have awakened the aspiration for birth into the Land of Bliss, if you continue saying the Name of Amida to the end of your life then, even though your mind strays while doing so, you will unfailingly attain birth.'

Ichigon Hōdan

Inferior practicers like myself are wholly incapable of ridding the heart and mind of distractions. Hence, without concern about whether we are agitated or not, we simply . . . say the Name. To wait expectantly for the moment the mind is concentrated would mean never being able to say it.

MYŌHEN

Nothing is of greater moment than realising that birth in the Land of Bliss is simple. Here, in essence, lies the central point of the Pure Land way. When you become aware of the ease of attaining birth, then it is indeed so. Nevertheless, modern scholars have produced a hodge-podge of conflicting doctrines and, because of the profundity of the sacred teaching, it is now all but impossible to distinguish true from erroneous.

ZENSHŌ

When you come to a landing just as a ferry is pulling away, there is only one thing to be done: simply grab hold and get aboard. If the crossing you seek traverses the river of passions surging through this life, then once you have encountered Amida's Name there is nothing else to be done: just say the *nembutsu*, reverently entrusting yourself to it. None of us fully realise how much we suffer because of our own calculating wisdom.

KENSHŌ

You may not go to great lengths to aid others but, if you truly aspire to part from samsaric existence, there is certain to be appropriate benefit for every other being.

MYŌZEN

Our pronouncing the Buddha's Name . . . or our thinking of him is not an act originating in ourselves but the act of Amida Buddha himself.

Anjin-ketsujō-shō

The way to say the *nembutsu* lies in having no 'way.' If you just say it earnestly, without taking account of your conduct or the good and bad in your heart, you will attain birth.

HŌNEN

When Amida willed to have his Name fill the world, his idea was to rouse his own image in the heart of every being. When the individual devotee responds to the call of Amida, who is the Buddha of Infinite Light and Eternal Life, their faith is confirmed and the assurance of rebirth in Amida's land is attained. This is deep calling unto deep.

D. T. SUZUKI

IMMEASURABLE LIFE

Although the one moment of *shinjin* and the one moment of *nembutsu* are two, there is no *nembutsu* separate from *shinjin*, nor is the one moment of *shinjin* separate from the one moment of *nembutsu*. . . . *Nembutsu* and *shinjin*, on our part, are themselves a manifestation of the Vow.

Shinran

On his way back from a pilgrimage to Zenkōji temple, Bishop Myō-hen of Mount Kōya had an interview with Hōnen. Myōhen asked, 'How can I break the bonds of samsaric existence with this life?' Hōnen replied, 'Just say the *nembutsu*.' 'That's surely the answer. But what should I do about the delusional thoughts and feelings that fill my mind?' 'Even though deluded thoughts arise, you will attain birth though the power of the Primal Vow.' Satisfied with this answer, Myōhen left. Afterwards Hōnen murmured to himself, 'Trying to attain the Pure Land by suppressing delusional thoughts is like casting away the eyes and nose you're born with in order to say the Name.'

Ichigon Hōdan

People unable to maintain the truth, as it demands, all surrender to their hearts and, in the end, come to give scarcely a thought to the world beyond. Taking the truth in vain—failing to carry it through to the end—is the greatest obstruction to birth. Whether you live a mundane life or for transcendence of this world, in the end the one great matter is death alone. Just resolve, 'When the time comes, so be it' and every pressing concern will vanish.

Kyōbutsu

Put plainly, if in your heart you genuinely aspire for the Pure Land and reject this defiled world, you will unfailingly attain birth by just saying the Name without any special concentration. If your aspiration is not authentic, you may clear away a hundred thousand obscurities and grasp the deepest of doctrinal truths, yet attainment of birth will elude you. In practicing the Buddha Way, continuous effort is crucial. It is preposterous for people who have once discerned their own capacities, and resolved upon the single practice of the *nembutsu*, to change because someone has spoken against it.

Myōhen

To speak deeply about the meaning of the *nembutsu* is, on the contrary, a sign of shallowness. Even though your reasoning does not go deep, if only your aspiration is so, you are certain to attain birth.

HŌNEN

Reliance on 'Other-Power' will remain unrealisable so long as the egocentric consciousness is being mistaken for the real person; it is this confusion of identity which the great *upāya**** propounded by Hōnen and Shinran was providentially designed to dispel. Let *nembutsu* serve as our perpetual defence against this fatal error, through the remembrance it keeps alive in human hearts.

MARCO PALLIS

When we entrust ourselves to the *Tathāgata*'s Primal Vow, we, who are like bits of tile and pebbles, are turned into gold . . . because we are taken into the heart of the Buddha of Unhindered Light.

SHINRAN

In the voice reciting the *nembutsu*, there is the light of Amida Buddha . . . a saving boat taking us to the golden shore where there is the consummation of happiness.

Kashiwazaki (Japanese *Noh* play)

In praise of Buddha:
The sun of his wisdom lights a thousand worlds;
His merciful clouds all creatures hide.
A myriad destinies are fulfilled in his love;
The voice of his Law—how it strikes my heart!

EMPRESS KŌKEN

Extraordinarily rare are those who, casting aside the desires and ambitions that torment the spirit, seek to devote themselves wholly to saying the Name with their hearts and minds unadorned, just as they are. . . . Do we realise what power is embodied in the mystery of Amida Buddha's Primal Vow? We are all busy fashioning our places in the world, neither reflecting on . . . our existence nor turning a

---

* Skillful means or saving stratagem.

thought to the power of the Buddha and the Dharma. Thus our karma runs on unchecked. This is a miserable attitude.

KENSHŌ

It is told: Bishop Eshin made a pilgrimage to the Great Shrine at Ise to spend seven days in secluded prayer. During the final night, in a dream, the portals of the holy shrine suddenly opened and a gentle-woman stepped forth in an aura of sanctity. She declared:

> The Goddess of the Great Shrine has returned to the capital, the primal enlightenment. I am caretaker in her absence. Instructions were left, saying: *If sentient beings of the last age should seek the essential path of liberation, advise them to say the Name of Amida Buddha.*

Ichigon Hōdan

The *Dharmakāya*, as the ground-reality, is *Mahāprajña* ('Great Wisdom') and Amida Buddha, as its active demonstration, is *Mahā-karuna* ('Great Compassion'). . . . Those not endowed with the religious 'eye' are blind to the tireless efforts of this Truth to demonstrate and make manifest its reality.

WASUI TATSUGUCHI

The sadness we feel at the moment of separation is fleeting, like a dream in the spring night. Whether we trust each other or revile each other now, let those who may be born in the Pure Land sooner show the way to those who come later. To become one who leads others to the Pure Land is a pleasure for those who are born there.

HŌNEN

Amida's Name is heard because the devotee has something to respond to it, and this something must be of the same order as Amida himself, otherwise there cannot be a response in any sense.

D. T. SUZUKI

This aspiration for Buddhahood is none other than the wish to save all beings. The wish to save all beings is the wish to carry all beings across the great ocean of birth-and-death . . . it is the aspiration to bring all beings to the attainment of supreme *Nirvāṇa*; it is the heart of great love and great compassion . . . which arises from the wisdom of immeasurable light.

SHINRAN

Amitābha is our universal self. And our desire for knowledge and illimitable life proves that, as a stone in obedience to the law of gravity strives towards the centre of the earth, so we feel ourselves eternally attracted to, and ever being drawn towards, the infinite being, *Amitābha*, who is the heart of the world.

RYŌTAI HATANI

Amida Buddha, as the personal manifestation of the *Dharmakāya*, is the source and sustainer of all being and the highest value of existence. . . . The person who has truly found Amida Buddha has found the ultimate basis that is great and powerful enough to order all their emotions and thoughts.

WASUI TATSUGUCHI

In short, out of the Absolute Buddha, or *Dharmakāya*, has the Buddha of salvation appeared and naturally, the spirit of Amida is in deep and intimate communion with the Absolute itself. And on our side, as we are also sharers in the being of the Absolute Buddha, we and Amida must be said to be one in substance, only differing in function.

SHŪGAKU YAMABE

It is an undeniable fact of life that all those who meet must one day part. And this state of affairs did not begin today. So let us not be anxious or sorrowful. If the conditions created by our past actions are sufficient, we shall be reborn on the same lotus blossom in the Land of Bliss.

HŌNEN

Amida Buddha is the basically real, purposive and energetic basis for all that is, save the free actions of beings of whom he is the foundation. According to Shin thinking, Amida Buddha is understood to be the ground of the universe, possessing all the known attributes of matter and mind. As such, Amida Buddha is not a disembodied spirit exercising some indefinable kind of authority upon a being he somehow created out of nothing. Rather, the very karmic process of the universe is Amida Buddha in action. The universe as we discern it is thought to be a part of the activity of Amida Buddha.

WASUI TATSUGUCHI

The path of sages belongs to a bygone era and is not suited to people of the present day. On the other hand, though the Pure Land path seems shallow at first glance, it is perfectly suited to the needs of ordinary, ignorant people like us.

HŌNEN

The Name is the bridge spanning the chasm between Amida and sentient beings.

D. T. SUZUKI

When a deer is being pursued by hunters, it does not stop even to look around for its fellows or look back at its pursuers but, with all eagerness, hastens straight forward and, no matter how many may be following, it escapes in safety. It is with the same determination that someone fully entrusts themselves to the Buddha's power and, without regard to anything else, steadfastly sets their mind upon being born in the Pure Land.

HŌNEN

From the very beginning sentient beings, who are filled with blind passions, lack a true mind and a heart of purity, for they are possessed of defilements and wrong views. Entrusting is to be free of doubt, believing deeply and without any double-mindedness in the *Tathāgata's* Primal Vow. This entrusting with sincere mind, then, is that arising from the Vow in which Amida urges every being throughout the ten directions: 'Entrust yourself to my Vow, which is true and real'; it does not arise from the hearts and minds of foolish beings of self-power.

SHINRAN

Do not be worrying as to whether your passions are strong or otherwise, or whether your faults are light or heavy. Only invoke Amida's name with your lips, and let the conviction accompany the sound of your voice, that you will of a certainty be born into the Pure Land.

HŌNEN

Rivers of blind passions, on entering the ocean—
The great, compassionate Vow
Of unhindered light filling the ten quarters—
Become one in taste with that sea of wisdom.

SHINRAN

There is no heart far from Amida, but a covered bowl of water cannot reflect the moon.

RENNYO

As a sound ship may carry a heavy load of stone thousands of miles across the ocean without sinking, likewise the weight of a person's offences, no matter how heavy, can cross to the other shore on the vessel of Amida Buddha's compassion. So, even if you have accumulated [many] misdeeds, do not doubt the power of the Primal Vow. This is called birth into the Pure Land through the power of the Other.

HŌNEN

From time immemorial, you . . . have been floundering in the realms of *saṃsāra*, undergoing indescribable troubles and afflictions. Until you were born in this life, you, too, underwent endless cycles of birth-and-death. Now you have encountered a Buddha and listened to his expositions of the Dharma. What pleasure and joy this is for you and for me to share. . . . In the life to come, you will be born in the land of *Amitāyus* ('Buddha of Immeasurable Life') and enjoy endless bliss there. Being forever in accord with the Way, you will . . . be free of the afflictions caused by greed, anger and stupidity. . . . You will dwell in effortless spontaneity and attain *Nirvāṇa*. You should each diligently seek to realise your aspiration. Do not entertain any doubt or give up your endeavour.

Sūtra on the Buddha of Immeasurable Life

O mist of spring, you hide all things beautiful and bright,
As if there did not shine the true, imperishable light.

HŌNEN

The Absolute Buddha, from which Amida manifests, is called the *Dharmakāya*. It is the source of all beings. It is the universal law by which all things exist. Nothing exists without it. Amida and all individual beings are two polar aspects of the Absolute Buddha.

RYUCHI FUJII

Pine of a thousand earthly years, I dwell beneath your shade,
Till by the Lord of Boundless Life, my welcome home is made.

HŌNEN

The present age is that of the decadent dharma and is riddled with defilements. Only the Pure Land is open to us.... All beings are unable to gauge their own capacities.... If we speak of the wrongdoings they commit, how do they differ from violent winds or tempests? For this reason, Buddhas—out of great compassion—have urged us to take refuge in the Pure Land. Even if you have committed many misdeeds throughout your life, concentrate your mind and diligently practice the *nembutsu* always. All your hindrances will, naturally, then be removed and you will definitely attain birth there.

TAO-CH'O

Shinjin is the source of enlightenment, the mother of virtues;
It nurtures all forms of goodness.
It cuts away the net of doubt and breaks free from the currents of desire;
It unfolds the supreme enlightenment of *Nirvāṇa*.
Shinjin harbours no defiled thoughts, it is pure,
Eradicating all arrogance; it is the root of reverence....
Shinjin gives freely and ungrudgingly;
Shinjin makes wisdom and virtues increase....
Shinjin purifies the faculties, makes them clear and sharp;
Its power is firm and steadfast, nothing can destroy it.

Avataṃsaka Sūtra

At the moment persons encounter Amida's Vow—which is Other-Power giving itself to us—and the heart that receives true *shinjin*, and rejoices, becomes settled in them, they are grasped, never to be abandoned.

SHINRAN

The evil will be saved and the virtuous, embraced, by Amida Buddha; the bad will be saved and the good, embraced; those who live afar will be saved and those who live near, embraced; those who live long after Shakyamuni's entrance into *Nirvāṇa* will be saved and those who live shortly after, embraced. The profundity and extensiveness of the great compassionate Primal Vow are beyond verbal description. Believe in them in the depth of your heart and validate the truth within yourself.... Amida Buddha does not abandon the most vile of men who have committed the [worst] offenses; He most certainly would not abandon us.

HōNEN

Even though the mind of faith is shallow, anyone who takes refuge in Amida will unfailingly attain birth, because the Primal Vow is deep. Even though the *nembutsu* may come from a reluctant heart, anyone who recites it never fails to see Amida welcoming him to his Pure Land; so great is the merit of the *nembutsu*. For this reason, we should rejoice at having encountered the Primal Vow.... Delusion is the nature of ordinary beings; apart from it, there is no mind in us. If we recite the *nembutsu*, while resigned to the fact that we are to remain ordinary beings full of delusion until death, we shall be received in welcome by Amida; then, as soon as we mount the lotus seat, our mind of delusion will be turned into that of enlightenment.

GENSHIN

The reason why Shin puts great stress on the sinful life of relative beings is to make them thus turn towards Amida and his Land.

D. T. SUZUKI

As I reverently reflect, I see that Shakyamuni exhorts us on this shore and that Amida, from that land, comes to welcome us. From there we are beckoned, from here we are urged on; how could we refuse to go? Just earnestly devote yourself to this dharma with life's limit as the end, and abandoning completely this defiled existence, immediately realise the eternal bliss of dharma-nature.

SHAN-TAO

Buddha of 'Immeasurable Light': because it cannot be calculated. Buddha of 'Boundless Light': because there is nothing on which it does not shine. Buddha of 'Unhindered Light': because, with regard to human beings and things, there is nothing that obstructs it. . . . Buddha of the 'Light of Purity': because it is manifested from good roots free of greed and rids sentient beings of their defilements. Buddha of the 'Light of Joy': because it arises from good roots free of anger, and can thus rid sentient beings of rage. Buddha of the 'Light of Wisdom': because, emerging from a mind of good roots free from folly, it rids sentient beings of ignorance. Buddha of 'Uninterrupted Light': because the Buddha's eternal light constantly illuminates and benefits beings. . . . That they are all touched by this light is due to the working of the 'Vow of softness and gentleness in body and mind.'

KYEONG-HEUNG

For a foolish being full of blind passions, in this fleeting world—this burning house—all matters without exception are lies and gibberish, totally without truth and sincerity. The *nembutsu* alone is true and real.

SHINRAN

Because the Sun of the *Tathāgata*'s Wisdom shines upon the darkness of karma-sooted sentient beings and, although it is impossible to eliminate the karma of birth-and-death, the Light of Amida that knows no hindrance . . . works to take up such beings. Therefore, without changing one thing about the nature of ignorance and bewilderment, we are surely brought to birth in the Pure Land of Wisdom.

ZONKAKU

The world seems a patchy, uneven affair but, outside that one total moment of enlightenment which Amida contributes to our welfare, there is not the smallest bit of input from the side of the seeker.

Anjin-ketsujō-shō

Birth in the Pure Land will never depend upon our goodness or lack thereof. It is possible solely through the power of the Primal Vow. No matter how brilliant and admirable we may be, it is extremely difficult during this age of the Decline of the Dharma to be born immediately into the Pure Land through one's own efforts. . . . There is no reason that even one who is unvirtuous, simple and incompetent cannot attain birth in the Pure Land. The essential condition is whether we believe in the Primal Vow of Amida Buddha.

HŌNEN

The *nembutsu* . . . is not a practice or a good act. Since it is not performed out of one's own design, it is not a practice. Since it is not
good done through one's own calculation, it is not a good act.
Because it arises wholly from Other-Power and is free of self-power
. . . it is neither a practice nor a good act.*

SHINRAN

As there is none lower than us as far as our ability as seekers go, we
should not look down upon others, yet it is these seekers of lesser
potential that Buddha sets out to save out of compassion. Though we
are cavalier in our efforts at practice, we must never harbour
doubt. . . . If one believes in the Primal Vow and says the Name, in
that moment one's birth is secure. But as we have no way of knowing
when a person's salvation has really been worked out . . . we may
think everything is all but certain, but the Buddha knows better and,
in the long run, the Buddha will certainly illumine that person.

ZONKAKU

Once you realise that the Name is not someone else's business, that
the Name is what has already completed the matter of our birth . . .
this is what is really meant by our 'hearing the Name.'

Anjin-ketsujō-shō

The uncrossable sea is the great sea of birth-and-death, and whether
one lives an ordinary life or treads the sacred path of the monastic, it
is far from easy for anyone to traverse it. Whatever practice I apply
myself to, whatever ship I may board, I run straight into a sheer cliff
in my attempt to cross that sea. Even though the desire to leave
behind the cycle of birth-and-death may burn in our breast, it is
impossible for us to realise that wish, . . . we people of the present
final age who represent humankind at the lowest rung of spiritual
ability! . . . Thus the *Tathāgata* gave rise to the vow of Great Compas-

---

* "Shinran advises his followers, 'Simply entrust yourself to the *Tathāgata*' or 'Simply entrust yourself to the power of the Vow' yet, in his writings, there is no instruc-
tion concerning how one should do this and no description of a general process
that results in the realisation of *shinjin*. This is to be expected; were there some
course of action to be fulfilled in order to attain *shinjin*, it would become our own
practice, subject to our deliberation and design." (Yoshifumi Ueda and Dennis
Hirota, *Shinran: An Introduction to His Thought*, pp. 158–59)

sion and Great Pity.... Truly this is the great ship taking us across that uncrossable sea, truly this is the epitome of the Universal Vow difficult to conceive! And not a whit of this do we owe to the efforts of the seeker; all of it comes about solely through the efforts that the Buddha's Vow makes for our sake.

ZONKAKU

Though we call the present world 'the last dharma-age of defilement and confusion,' Amida's Primal Vow is mysteriously thriving all the more. Therefore, lay people must understand that unless they rely on this vast, compassionate Vow, realise the one thought-moment* of faith, and attain birth in the Pure Land of Suchness (eternity and bliss), it is indeed as if they went to a mountain of treasure and returned empty-handed. Quieten your minds and deeply reflect on this.

RENNYO

Amida Buddha is...none other than this act (*nembutsu*). It is through the effect of this act on us that we can say that our birth is a certainty. Thus even when the spiritually ungifted call to Buddha in their distracted state of mind, this meets the full requirements of the Vow. This should make us aware that this act of the Vow is not being initiated from the side of the seeker.

Anjin-ketsujō-shō

Sentient beings are bound up by all kinds of karmic obstruction, and are incarcerated in this prison cell of the world, where they are bound by the effects of all kinds of actions, making them unable to achieve liberation from the cycle of birth-and-death.... So deeply defiled is the ordinary person by hindrances dragging them down, they can

---

* "This 'one moment' (*ichinen*) is not just another moment in the conventional sense; it is the shortest possible instant of time and thus is both time at its threshold and beyond time. It is in such a point of time that the 'heart-water' of sentient beings, whether good or bad, returns to and enters the ocean of the Vow (Buddha's heart and mind) and becomes one in taste with it. Here, in other words, occurs the oneness of the mind of the foolish being and the mind of Buddha. The oneness or single taste of time and the timeless that takes place here constitutes the essence of *shinjin*. Thus, the moment of awakening *shinjin* and saying the *nembutsu* is a moment both in and out of time. It is time that has become full and rich, having been permeated by timelessness." (*The Collected Works of Shinran*, vol. 2, p. 197)

hardly expect to escape the consequence of further transmigration.... But if we put our lives in the hands of the Other-Power, if we
count on the Buddha's Vow ... we forever depart the castle of suffering ... where we have long been interred, and at last we arrive at the
Pure Land emptied of such karma.

ZONKAKU

In this world (the Pure Land)...there is pleasure without end.
Human beings and heavenly beings mingle with and see each other. All
have a mind of compassion and they mutually love one another....
For every desire, there is something to satisfy it and there is nothing
which does not appease the heart.... There is not the pain of parting
from loved ones which causes an ever-increasing sadness.... Nor is
there any pain of hatred or envy, for they look upon each other with
eyes of mercy and with a heart of sympathy.

GENSHIN

Although they neither seek nor know the indescribable, inexplicable,
and inconceivable virtues of the Pure Land of happiness, those who
entrust themselves to the Primal Vow are made to acquire them.

SHINRAN

In this Land, there is no suffering of any kind; in this Land, there is
only happiness.

Smaller Sūtra on the Buddha of Immeasurable Life

In that realm, the joy acquired reaches its highest consummation. As
humans and gods intermingle, while each remains who they are, they
are able to peer into each other's world. Perfumed by a compassionate
heart, it is as if they see in one another their only child, and together
(as mother and child) they roam the breadth of that azure land, playing together in its sandalwood groves, going from one palace to the
next, visiting one sheltered oasis after another. And if they so desire it
be quiet, the sounds of winds and waves will naturally drift away from
their ears, and if they desire to cast their eyes upon something grand,
vistas of mountains and streams and plunging gorges will summarily
arise before their very eyes. All their other functions such as smelling
and touching, as well as thinking, will arise in accordance with their
wishes.... The truth is, as they are in the state of non-retrogression

(and cannot fall back into *saṃsāra*) ... and as their lives are infinite, they will never experience the suffering of birth, ageing, infirmity and death. As their hearts are perfectly matched with Reality, they will never experience the suffering of having to part from a loved one.*

ZONKAKU

The mind that aspires to attain Buddhahood is the mind to save all sentient beings. The mind to save all sentient beings is the mind to grasp and bring them to birth in the land where the Buddha is. Thus, the person who aspires to be born in the Pure Land of happiness must unfailingly awaken the mind aspiring for supreme enlightenment. Suppose there is a person who, without awakening this mind, simply hears that bliss is enjoyed in that land without interruption and desires to be born there for the sake of the bliss; such a person will not be able to attain birth. Thus it is said, 'They do not seek the sustained bliss for their own sake, but think only of freeing all sentient beings from pain.' 'Sustained bliss' means that the Pure Land of happiness is sustained by the power of Amida's Primal Vow, and that the enjoyment of bliss is without interruption.

T'AN-LUAN

When we come to know truly that we are possessed of blind passions,
And entrust ourselves to the power of the Primal Vow,
We will, on abandoning completely our defiled existence,
Realise the eternal bliss of Dharma-nature.

SHINRAN

When a believer is born into the Pure Land ... all their pleasures are increased a hundred thousand times above what they were before. Such a person is like a blind man who has, for the first time, received his sight or like a man from the country who has suddenly been transported to a palace. As he looks at his own body, his skin becomes radiant with golden rays. ... As he beholds the radiance of the Buddha, his eyes become purified and he is able to see the multitudes that

---

* As already mentioned in the introduction, the descriptions, in this and similar passages, which suggest a quasi-material paradise should be taken as metaphorical; that is, as a figurative approach to spiritual reality under the guise of concrete forms. In this way, a state which is—properly speaking—ineffable is conveyed to ordinary minds in such a way as to heighten our aspiration for it.

assemble in the next world. Everything of form and sound is mysterious and marvellous to him. When he looks up into the spacious sky, he beholds a wide radiance of sublimity so glorious that heart and words cannot express it, and his eyes lose themselves in the path of clouds.

GENSHIN

The Land of Bliss is the true and real land of no-self, so birth there is altogether unattainable through good acts performed with self-attachment in self-power. It can be realised only through the single practice of the all-encompassing Vow. Foolish beings, then, cannot be born through their own will and aspiration. To pursue various aspirations instead of saying the Name, to the very end of life, is to be ignorant of the true and real Buddha-dharma and thus be unable to attain birth.

IPPEN

It has been said that those who do not know the importance of the afterlife are foolish, even though they may understand eighty thousand sutras and teachings; those who know about the afterlife are wise even though they may be unlettered men and women who have renounced the world while remaining in lay life. The import of our tradition is, therefore, that for those who do not realise the significance of the one thought-moment of faith—even though they may diligently read the various scriptures and be widely informed—all is in vain.

RENNYO

Extremely difficult is it to encounter an age in which a Buddha appears, and difficult indeed for a person to realise the wisdom of *shinjin*. To come to hear the dharma rarely met with is again among all things most difficult. To realise *shinjin* oneself and to guide others to *shinjin* is among difficult things yet even more difficult. To awaken beings everywhere to great compassion is truly to respond in gratitude to the Buddha's benevolence.

SHAN-TAO

Being born in the Pure Land means, first, recalling it as your homeland. To do so, let your thoughts dwell deeply on the truth of the Vow.

HŌNEN

IMMEASURABLE LIFE

Why do you not diligently practice good, reflect on the naturalness of the Way and realise that it is above all discriminations and boundlessly pervasive? You should each make a great effort to attain it. Strive to escape from *saṃsāra* and be born in the Land of Peace and Provision. . . . The Pure Land is easy to reach, but very few actually go there. It rejects nobody, but naturally and unfailingly attracts beings. Why do you not abandon worldly matters and strive to enter the Way?

Sūtra on the Buddha of Immeasurable Life

After you have gained *shinjin*, even when you hear the same teaching again, you should feel as if it was for the first time. People only wish to hear something new. However many times you may hear the same teaching, you ought to think that this is a rare and marvellous thing which you have never heard before.

RENNYO

Aspire for the attainment of birth [in the Pure Land] by unfailingly and decidedly taking as essential the Vow directed to you from the true and real mind. This mind, in its profound entrusting, is like a diamond; it is not shaken, confused, defeated, or broken by people of other views, other teachings, different understandings, or different practices. Just be decisively settled, single-heartedly hold to the Vow, and rightly and directly go forward, without paying attention to what others may say. If your heart advances and retreats, and you look back with weak and cowardly thoughts, you will fall from the path and forfeit the great benefit of birth.

SHAN-TAO

Ah, hard to encounter, even in many lifetimes, is the decisive cause of birth, Amida's universal vow! . . . Wholly sincere, indeed, are the words of truth that one is grasped, never to be abandoned—the right dharma all-surpassing and wondrous! Hear and reflect, and let there be no wavering or apprehension.

SHINRAN

How gracious is Amida *Tathāgata*'s light! Without encountering the [receptive] condition of this light, there can be no cure at all for the fearful sickness of ignorance and karma-hindrance, which has been ours from the beginningless past. Prompted by the condition of this light, and with the ripening of good from the past, we assuredly attain

Other-Power faith now. It is immediately clear, however, that this is faith granted by Amida. Hence we know now, beyond question, that this is not faith generated by the practicer. Accordingly, all those who have once attained Other-Power faith should reflect gratefully on the *Tathāgata*'s benevolence and repeat the *nembutsu*, saying the Name of the Buddha always.

RENNYO

When *shinjin* emerges in us . . . we find ourselves saying the *nembutsu*, and also [being enfolded] by the radiant Light that receives all.

KAKUNYO

There are innumerable modes of entry into the Buddha's teaching. Just as there are in the world difficult and easy paths—travelling on foot by land is full of hardship and travelling in a boat by sea is pleasant—so it is among the paths of the bodhisattvas. Some engage in rigorous practice and endeavour; others quickly reach the stage of non-retrogression through the easy practice of entrusting as the means [for attaining it].

NĀGĀRJUNA

With all the merits of worship and repentance, at the time of death, I wish to see the body of the Buddha of Infinite Life. May I, and other aspirants, behold the Buddha, acquire the eye of non-defilement, be born in the Land of Peace and Bliss, and realise the supreme enlightenment.

SHAN-TAO

The Pure Land has been established to engender in us a longing for it and to encourage us to aspire for birth there. And our longing is aroused, in short, so that we say the Name. . . . As we hear of the wondrousness of the Pure Land, aspiration for birth naturally awakens in us. When this aspiration has arisen, the Name unfailingly comes to be uttered.

IPPEN

The pronouncing of the Name is possible only when Amida 'within us', so to speak, is awakened from the darkness of ignorance. When the latter event does not take place, the pronouncing of the Name is mere shadow with nothing really backing it; there is no correspondence between reality and expression, between content and form, between heart and lips.

D. T. SUZUKI

Needless to say, our Buddha Amida grasps beings with the Name. Thus, as we hear it with our ears and say it with our lips, exalted virtues without limit grasp and pervade our hearts and minds. It becomes ever after the seed of our Buddhahood.

YUAN-CHAO

Amida's light illumines the person of true *shinjin* always, without interruption, at all times and places . . . hence the darkness of ignorance has already been cleared, and the long night of birth-and-death is already dispelled to dawn. Let this be known.

SHINRAN

While reciting the *nembutsu* we must arouse in ourselves profound faith, loathe this defiled world of suffering and long for the Land of Ultimate Bliss.

HŌNEN

There is no set number of times the Name must be said and . . . no determined hour or occasion for saying it. Since we have been given this Vow by the *Tathāgata*, we can take any occasion in daily life for saying the Name and need not wait to recite it at the very end of our lives. . . . When persons realise this true and real *shinjin* (entrusting), they enter completely into the compassionate light that grasps, never to abandon, and hence become established in the stage of the truly settled.

SHINRAN

Those who accept the *nembutsu* in faith, however well versed in the lifetime teachings of the Buddha, should consider themselves as illiterate, stupid persons, and without pretensions to wisdom; they should single-heartedly recite the *nembutsu* with ordinary Buddhist devotees of little learning, whether men or women.

HŌNEN

The repeated pronouncing of Amida's Name, however mechanical and contentless in the beginning, gradually sets up a process of rearrangement in the consciousness of the practiser who becomes thus unwittingly aware of the presence of Amida in their own inner being. When this moment is realised, they utter for the first time—from the depths of their soul—the Name of Amida as the power lifting them from the burden of karma. . . . The psychological tone of consciousness created by continuous recitation will one day, when time matures, prepare the way for the devotee to awaken faith in Amida.

D. T. SUZUKI

Without deliberating, or designing in any way at all, entrust yourself to the Primal Vow and say the *nembutsu*. Whether you say it with your mind firmly settled or not, the *nembutsu* cannot deviate from the all-surpassing . . . Other-Power. In Amida's Primal Vow there is nothing lacking, nothing superfluous. Beyond this, what is there to say? Just return to the mind and heart of a simple, foolish person and say the *nembutsu*.

IPPEN

Amida is conceived as a person embodying the absolute truth in its highest form . . . and as the culmination of our religious yearnings.

SHŪGAKU YAMABE

In entrusting ourselves to the *Tathāgata*'s Primal Vow and saying the Name once we, necessarily, without seeking it, are made to receive the supreme virtues and, without knowing it, we acquire the great and vast benefit. . . . The boundlessness, expansiveness, and all-inclusiveness of the *Tathāgata*'s virtues is likened to the unobstructed fullness of the waters of a great ocean.

SHINRAN

Amida Buddha does not discriminate between one who observes the precepts and one who violates them. Nor does he discriminate between the poor and the wealthy, and pays no regard to social class. His power changes our karmic nature, like a stone or tile turned into gold. Through the *nembutsu*, Amida also promised that he will come to welcome all devotees without exception.

HŌNEN

IMMEASURABLE LIFE

Treat the Buddha-Dharma as your master and secular matters as your guests. After you have established your faith in the Buddha-Dharma, you should treat secular matters as you see fit.

RENNYO

Know that the person who utters the *nembutsu* is a white lotus among people.

Sūtra of Contemplation on the Buddha of Immeasurable Life

Before one comes to the awareness of absolute dependence, one has to undergo much inner struggle; the realisation of *tariki* is never attained until the last straw of self-assertion is given up. Passivity marks the end of the utmost strenuousness and tension. Without the latter, no *tariki* experience will take place in anybody's spiritual life.

D. T. SUZUKI

The mind that aspires to attain Buddhahood is the mind to save all sentient beings; the mind to save all sentient beings is true and real *shinjin*, which is Amida's benefiting of others. . . . *Shinjin* is the mind that is single; the mind that is single is the diamond-like mind. The diamond-like mind is the mind aspiring for enlightenment; this mind is itself Other-Power.

SHINRAN

How sad sentient beings are, as if inchworms going round in circles or as if silkworms tying themselves up with their own threads. How sad the lives of sentient beings who . . . are upside-down due to their attachment to impurities. Generating a place where there is no falsity . . . or transmigration, the Buddha aspires to benefit sentient beings by giving them a great realm of ultimate purity, peace and sustenance.

ZONKAKU

The Name of Amida's unique, all-surpassing Vow
Embodies the inconceivable working of Other-Power;
When you just say this Name, leaving everything to your lips,
In that voicing, all your transgressions in the realm of birth-and-death vanish.

IPPEN

With pity, Amida fixes his attention on us so that his mind-and-heart penetrates as deep as the marrow of our bones and stays there. It is like a piece of charcoal that has caught fire. We cannot pluck the fire from the burning charcoal however much we try. . . . Even though it is contaminated with the three poisons of greed, hatred and illusion . . . there is no region of our heart that is not saturated with the Buddha's virtue. Thus the Buddha and sentient beings constitute one body from the very beginning. This state of unity is called *Namu Amida Butsu.*

Anjin-ketsujō-shō

Know that Amida Buddha is light and that light is the form taken by Wisdom.

SHINRAN

The sorrow of impermanence that descends upon us cannot be avoided outside the Pure Land. Yet it is impossible to transcend our bodies that depend on material things to exist, unless we leave behind the cycle of birth-and-death. . . . If we set ourselves in good stead with Amida's Vow Power, we realise that our birth in the Land of Peace and Sustenance is secure, as this Land is itself the realm of eternal *Nirvāṇa*. It is a world wherein we do not grow weary, a world wherein we do not revert to our former state. Because of this, without having to resort to our own clever actions, we can pin ourselves onto the sleeves of the Buddha to forever avoid the Wheel of Impermanence of birth-and-death, and reach the vaunted plane of true Permanence.

Nirvāṇa Sūtra

The spirit of the Pure Land school is that it is basically for *bombu* (ordinary people) and not for saints. However, unless what the Buddha taught was false, we must conclude that impending birth in the Pure Land most decidedly awaits the *bombu*, whose greed is profound, whose anger is fierce and whose ignorance smoulders, in this round of transmigration.

KAKUNYO

Shinjin is the aspiration to bring all beings to the attainment of supreme *Nirvāṇa*; it is the heart of great love and great compassion. This *shinjin* is Buddha-nature and Buddha-nature is *Tathāgata*. To realise this *shinjin* is to rejoice and be glad.

SHINRAN

IMMEASURABLE LIFE

In the so-called *jiriki* or self-power schools such as Shingon or Zen, the realisation of Buddhahood can, generally, only take place after long preparation in this life but, in Shin, it can be consummated only in the Pure Land after death and—unlike Zen—true enlightenment can never take place in this world.... The Pure Land is not to be regarded as a material paradise but as a positive *Nirvāṇa* ... it is conceived, not only as a land of happiness and peace, but as a field of enlightenment for the practice of *genso-eko* ('returning to this world') in order to help sentient beings.... The Pure Land is a place or condition of activity and not of negative rest.

D.T. Suzuki

Even though we recite [the *nembutsu*] and think on Amida, we do not thereby intend to amass merit but simply perform the practice which Amida has already accomplished for us ordinary people.

Anjin-ketsujō-shō

When shackled foolish beings—the lowly who are hunters and peddlers—wholly entrust themselves to the Name embodying great wisdom, the inconceivable Vow of the Buddha of Unhindered Light, then while burdened as they are with blind passion, they attain supreme *Nirvāṇa*.

Shinran

Even if we enjoy a life of pomp and glory and do as we wish, this is only a matter of some fifty to a hundred years. If the wind of impermanence were to come even now and summon us, would we not suffer illness of one kind or another and die? And indeed, at the time of death, neither family nor wealth, on which we have depended for so long, can accompany us.... Let us realise, then, that we should earnestly aspire to birth in the Pure Land in the afterlife, that the one we should rely upon is Amida *Tathāgata*, and that the place to which we should go, faith having been decisively settled, is the Pure Land of serene sustenance.

Rennyo

The background of *tariki* mysticism is deeply stained with blood and tears, and the doctrine of absolute passivity is heavily lined with the ugly wounds of merciless self-criticism.

D.T. Suzuki

The Supreme Buddha is formless and because of being formless is called *jinen.** When this Buddha is shown as being with form, it is not called the supreme *Nirvāṇa*. In order to make us realise that the true Buddha is formless, it is expressly called Amida Buddha; so I have been taught. Amida Buddha is the medium through which we are made to realise *jinen*.

SHINRAN

As I observe the present state of affairs, [it is clear that] because this is a time of instability, human sorrow exceeds all imagination. . . . Quite simply, where I am eager to be born is the Pure Land of utmost bliss, and what I aspire to and long to attain is the undefiled Buddha-body. . . . Existence is as ephemeral as a flash of lightning or the morning dew, and the wind of impermanence may blow even now. Yet we think only of prolonging this life for as long as possible, without ever aspiring for the afterlife. This is inexpressibly deplorable.

RENNYO

For the sake of our impending birth in the Pure Land, true entrusting (*shinjin*) comes first and foremost; pay no heed to the rest. When it comes to that one great matter of our birth, however, there is nothing that the *bombu* has to especially figure out; simply leave everything to the *Tathāgata*. . . . This is the seeker who, assenting to Other-Power, has actively received true entrusting.

KAKUNYO

When you meet a person distraught over the loss of someone dear, recommend to them the medicine of the Dharma; instruct and guide them in what Buddhism has to tell us at this impasse in our lives. Of the sufferings of the human realm, there is nothing more painful than that of having to leave our loved ones behind. First, tell them the plain truth: that, in this world of birth-and-death, there is no one who lives forever; next, explain to them the condition of the realm of peace and sustenance: that though we are now caught in misery and suffering, if

---

* "A term for the ultimate reality of Buddhism, expressing Suchness, or 'things-as-they-are', free from the bondage of birth-and-death. *Jinen* thus signifies that which is beyond form and time, and beyond the domain of human intellect and will. It is the Dharma-Body as Suchness, which 'fills the hearts and minds of the ocean of all beings.'. . ." (*The Collected Works of Shinran*, vol. 2, p. 191)

we do not aspire for the Pure Land, in future we shall again meet with grief and sorrow. On the other hand, when ... we turn to Amida's Pure Land and 'enter his *Nirvāṇa* Palace', in this new orientation to our life, the grief and sorrow of the darkness enshrouding us is cleared away and, without knowing it, we find ourselves being taken up and brought to benefit from the Light. ... Another name for wine is *bo-yu* meaning 'to forget your troubles.' Comfort the bereaved by having them partake of some wine, leaving them once their smiles have returned. This, then, is how we should treat those in mourning. Keep these points well in mind.

SHINRAN

Our life is Amida's life even while we are unaware of it. We do not know this while our wisdom is not yet developed.

Anjin-ketsujō-shō

There are other kinds of prayer besides mere asking for a favour or an intercession. When, for instance, prayer is the utterance of the suffering soul seeking to emancipate itself from the bondage of karma, or to be helped out of being hopelessly drowned in the ocean of its own sin, it is really of religious significance and in full accord with the spirit of the Shin teaching.

D. T. SUZUKI

The person who has attained true and real *shinjin* is taken into and protected by the Vow which grasps, never to abandon; therefore, they realise the diamond-like mind without any calculation on their part.[*]

SHINRAN

We leave the one great matter of our impending birth to the Buddha. However, the actions of our body, the drifts of our minds, the words of our mouths as the roots of the three poisons of greed, hatred and stupidity ... all make our defiled existence so difficult to rise above and make this realm so difficult to leave behind. For the foolish and spiritually inept who have only succeeded in filling their lives with

---

[*] "The negation of human calculation does not mean the negation of our efforts towards realisation; what is negated is the attachment to one's self—the thoughts, achievements and claims of the self-centred heart and mind." (Yoshifumi Ueda, *Letters of Shinran*, p. 68)

blind passion, it is truly wonderful that ... the very individuals for whom Amida made his true vow are simply those who are their unassuming selves, who do not pretend to be other than what they are.

KAKUNYO

It is indeed that sentient beings doubt what should not be doubted;
The Pure Land is right before us and never out of harmony with us.
Do not ponder whether Amida will take you in or not;
The question is whether or not you wholeheartedly turn about at heart.

SHAN-TAO

The act of saying the *nembutsu* is itself the fulfilment of Amida's Vow in us; therefore, the reciting act itself is proof of our deliverance.... Amida's Vow realises itself as our faith and, at the same time, that faith proves the presence of the Vow.

SHŌJUN BANDŌ

The name 'Amida' (*Amitābha* in Sanskrit) signifies Infinite Light, and it is the first axiom of Shin Buddhism that Amida sends out his light to illuminate this world. So wherever we see beauty, holiness, compassion or love manifested in our world of ignorance and illusion, we can know that it is because Amida's light is shining through the darkness.

BEATRICE LANE SUZUKI

APPENDIX

VOICES OF LIGHT

—Sayings of the Myōkōnin and Other Masters of the Inner Life

Introduction

A *myōkōnin* ('truly wondrous person') is someone who embodies certain virtues of character and faith that make them exemplars of the Shin Buddhist way of life. These include an unaffected but simple devotion, spontaneity of thought and action, a ruthless introspection and an other-worldliness that is yet bound up with a full engagement in life.

A number of them were illiterate and sometimes even eccentric or naïve in the ways of the world. This often manifested in a refreshing candour of expression coupled with penetrating spiritual insights. However, others were respected scholars with a lively intellectual manner that was always direct, unencumbered by academic pedantry.

The myōkōnin and other masters selected in the following pages are from the modern period and offer striking and deeply visceral declarations of their rich inner life. They epitomise a living and dynamic faith that is founded on an intimate relationship with Amida Buddha as a real person.

O-KARU (1801–1856)

Do you dislike
 Hearing the Truth?
What do you
 Truly desire?

How can I hear the truth
 By relying on 'self-power'?
All I do (by striving that way)
 Is expend myself
 Trying to satisfy
 Selfish desires.

Consider well
 While still alive.
When life ends,
 It is too late.

When Amida Buddha's mind
 Is realised,
No other striving
 Is required.

My heart is like a rough pine
 Lacking any polish,
Amida makes me the object of his concern
 All the more.

The voice heard yesterday
 And again today,
 Is Amida calling,
Calling to promise,
 Promising birth
 In his Pure Land.

Though we must live apart
 In this world. . . .
How pleasant to consider
 The land where we will
 Be together again.

How can I

Not be grateful?
Amida accepts me
   Naked,
   Just as I am.

Though my body
   Is clothed in rags,
My heart is adorned
   With a wadded silk garment
   When I hear
   Amida's teaching!

Though mocked in this world
   As a crazy old hag,
In the Pure Land
   I will be a radiant bride!

My inability to do anything to bring about
   my enlightenment. . . .
   That is why I am worthy of being 'saved.'
Amida's Imperial Order
   Is to come just I am.
Even this (strong-willed) O-Karu
   Cannot hold up her head.
I shall be taken
   As Amida wills.

Do not be deceived
   That there will be a tomorrow. . . .
For there is only today.

Amida's compassion
   Tenderly permeates
Every nook and corner—
   Particularly me!

How grateful I am!
   When I humbly look at myself,
I find there
   A plum brought to fruit against my will.

From the Capital of Flowers,
   How good of Amida

To have come in person,
  Unable to abandon me.

Please rejoice
  In Amida's compassion.
Do not think
  Life lasts forever.
My life is uncertain
  As is yours.

We live for just a night
  Here in a temporary dwelling.
Before returning
  To our Parent's home,
We are just doing our part
  In this world.

Though we will part,
  Life now is like a dream
  Of a single night:
Our minds soon will rest
  On the petals of a lotus. . . .

The Great Compassion
  Combs my tangled hair
So the heavy obstacles
  Barring my Buddhahood
Are no longer there. . . .

How grateful I am!
  Leaving it all to
  The wind of the Dharma,
I feel
  It is always spring.

I ask myself
  If I have a good heart,
But what I find
  Causes me only shame.

The picture of
  Amida printed
  On a silk fabric

VOICES OF LIGHT

Is the sound
  Of *Namu Amida Butsu*
Given form.

Seeing
  Beautiful flowers
  Out of season
I am brought to realise
  My limitedness. . . .

My understanding is like
  A light evening shower.
It does not begin to quench
  The parched earth.

A life of complaint
  Along a dark road of delusion,
Is now illuminated by
  Amida Buddha's constant light.

'O-Karu, O-Karu'
  Someone shakes me gently.
'Yes, yes, here I am',
  But even that reply
  Is really from you.

I am an ungrateful person
  Who feels
  Not the least indebted,
So Amida saves me
  Just as I am.

Just take the incomparably
  Superb jeweled medicine,
  The Name of Amida.
All darkness
  Will then be dispelled.

The five defilements[*]
  Cause me to drift

---

[*] These refer to the five corruptions in this mundane world: famine, pestilence, war, physical weakening and shortened life-span.

Under the dark moonless sky. . . .
But I am securely moored
  In the port of *Namu Amida Butsu.*

Even the crane
  Which lives
  A thousand years,
Gazes at the moon
  Through the branches
  Of pine trees.

I hear that
  An out-going breath
  Does not wait
  For an in-coming breath.
And so the traveller must hurry
  On their way to the Pure Land.

Though our minds
  Change from moment to moment,
The colour of flowers
  Remains the same.

After death
  Along with tears
  In the hereafter,
I take joy in
  The land of 'meeting again.'

Fish live in a shoal
  And birds in the woods.
I dwell within
  The six characters of
  Na-mu A-mi-da Butsu.

After I leave this world,
  If someone should ask for me,
Tell them I have gone to
  The Pure Land,
  The Pure Land
  Of my dear Amida Buddha.

VOICES OF LIGHT

Gōjun Shichiri (1835–1900)

To hear the call of Amida . . . ultimately comes down to uttering the one word 'Yes' in response. Don't say 'but' and get away from his universal embrace.

It is like the moon reflected in a tub. The harder we try to take hold of it, the more turbulent grows the water and the more disturbed the reflection. But by leaving it alone, the full moon serenely shines on the water. Just so, when we are too anxious to feel joyful, this defeats its own end. Better to have no such anxieties but simply believe in the efficacy of the Primal Vow and all that is needed for your happiness will follow by itself.

When the founder (Shinran) tells us to place reliance upon Amida, it means to make his power our own. It is like a child being carried on the back of its parent—the strength of the latter is the strength of the former.

In a poor family, there is but one coat for both father and son.

It is like throwing a handful of snow into boiling water; no trace of it will be visible in the cauldron. Let all the faith, all the joy, all the *nembutsu* that you can find in your heart be thrown into the pot of the Primal Vow, and you will find yourself in one water of identification.*

According to some teachings, good is practicable only after the eradication of evil. This is like trying to dispel the darkness first in order to let the light in.

You cannot stop deluded thoughts asserting themselves because they belong to the nature of common mortals.

When Amida's mercy is not taken into our own hearts and we only ask whether our doubt is cleared and faith is gained, this faith becomes a thing apart from mercy and one is set against the other. This we call a state of confusion.

* Note by D. T. Suzuki: *We must not, however, forget that with the Shin devotee, this 'one water of identification' is always described in terms of the Other and not 'I.'*

To 'hear' is the whole thing in the teaching of *tariki*; the sutra says, 'Hear the name of Amida.' The Buddha, let us observe, does not tell us to think, for hearing is believing and not thinking. How do we hear then? No special contrivance is needed; in thinking, we may need to adopt some method but hearing is just to receive what is given—there is no deliberation here.

If we have no inner sense of acceptance as to Amida's infinite grace, it is like listening to the sound of rice-pounding at your next door neighbour's which will never appease our own feeling of hunger.

Some say that Buddhism is pessimistic and does not produce beneficial results in our lives. But how could Buddhists be induced to love this world so full of evils?

Knowledge is the outcome of reasoning and knows no limit: faith is the truth of personality. Faith and knowledge are not to be confused.

Amida holds in his hands both love and knowledge for the salvation of sentient beings. So we read, 'In the depths of Amida's compassion there lies his wisdom beyond calculation.' *Namu Amida Butsu* signifies the union of love and wisdom, and is the free gift of Amida to us.

When we speak of Amida and sentient beings, they appear to be different, one from the other; but when such beings are thrown into the fire of mercy, they are one even with Amida himself. Like a piece of live charcoal—fire is charcoal and charcoal is fire; they cannot be separated.

To have 'faith' means not to have any doubt about the Primal Vow; when there is not the least shadow of a doubt about the Vow, other things will take care of themselves.

The principle of the *tariki* teaching is: 'Just ask and you will be saved' and not 'Do this and salvation will be its reward.' Nothing is imposed on you as the price of salvation. When you give sweets to your children, you do not tell them to do this or that; you simply give them away. Nothing is expected of them, for it is a free gift. With Amida, his gift has no conditions attached to it. Let your mortal weaknesses remain what they are and be absorbed in the infinite grace of Amida.

When faith gradually takes possession of our hearts, we will naturally cease from harmful or misguided behaviour. Through the grace of Amida, our lives will be made easier and happier.

Saké cannot be poured into an overturned cup but, when it stands in its natural position, anybody can pour saké into it as fully as it can hold. Therefore, have the cup of your heart upright, ready to receive and hear; it will surely be filled with Amida's mercy.

There are people who have heard of the Primal Vow and say they believe in it but, somehow, they feel uneasy when they think of their last moments. They are like those who, feeling dizzy at the surging billows, are not at all sure of their safety sailing over the ocean. If they are too frightened at the passions that are stirring in their hearts, which they think will assuredly interfere with their ultimate salvation, there will be no end to their vexations. Look at the spacious boat instead of the billows; for the boat is large and safe enough for every one of us, however sinful and numerous we are, and there will be no feeling of uneasiness left in us.

We must pay fair prices for things that belong to others. But when they are those of our own parents, they are justly ours too and we do not have to pay for them. This is because of the parental love that allows us to inherent all that belongs to us regardless of our capacities. So with Amida; he bestows upon us freely all that he has—and here is the secret of the *tariki* teaching.

ASAHARA SAICHI (1850–1932)

Death has been snatched away from me,
And, in its place, the *Namu Amida Butsu*.

The future destination that Amida Buddha
Has given to me is everlasting Happiness.
No more the tears and troubles of this tumultuous world.

O, Saichi, what is your pleasure? My pleasure is this world of delusion
Because it turns into the seed of delight in the Dharma.

How fine!
The whole world and vastness of space is Buddha!
And I am in it—*Namu Amida Butsu!*

I am a happy man,
A glad heart is given me;
Amida's gladness is my gladness.

How do you understand a life of gratitude?
As to being grateful, sometimes I remember it, sometimes I do not.
Really, a wretched man am I!

My birthplace? I am born of hell:
I am a nobody's dog
Carrying my tail between my legs;
I pass this world of woes,
Saying *Namu Amida Butsu*.

How grateful!
While others die,
I do not die:
Not dying, I go
To Amida's Pure Land.

The treasure of the six syllables was given to me by *Oya-sama**:

---

* *Oya-sama*: a more intimate reference to Amida Buddha; the word *oya* means
'parent' and *sama* is an honorific used to refer to someone towards whom one has
great respect or reverence.

VOICES OF LIGHT

However much one spends of it, it is never exhausted.
The treasure grows all the more as it is used;
It is the most wondrous treasure.

This old self of mine has so many delusions piled up;
So now I hand then over,
So now I hand them over,
So now I hand them over, to you;
Ah, what a great feeling!

You ensure me safe passage home from this floating world.
Your kindness is more than I deserve.
How my heart fills with joy.

The most wonderful thing is
That the Buddha's invisible heart of compassion is visible
While I'm right here.

How wretched!
And how joyous!
They are one
In *Namu Amida Butsu.*

When you catch a cold, a cough keeps coming up.
Saichi has caught the cold of Dharma,
And that cough of *nembutsu* keeps coming up again and again.

When I received the kindness of our *Oya*,
Truly I understood how false I was through and through.

Let this world go as it does,
Ignorance-debts, all paid up by *Nyorai-san.**
How happy, how happy I am!

Just as the sardine are hauled up and taken away
Out of the sea by the netful,
Me too—I was hauled up and taken away
By your net of compassion.

---

* *Nyorai* is the Japanese term for *Tathāgata*; *san* is an honorific suffix.

I received the eye to see Amida *from* Amida.

Saichi's heart, how miserable!
All kinds of delusion thickly arise all at once!
A hateful fire mixed with evils is burning,
How miserable! A fire mixed with follies is burning.
Saichi's heart, worrying,
A heart in utter confusion,
Saichi's heart rising as high as the sky!
When the *bombu* is not understood
It is wickedness;
When understood, it is humility.
Saichi's heart is all rain,
Saichi's heart, like rain and rain, is all rain;
Saichi's heart is all fog, like fog within a fog. . . .
They understand who have had sorrows,
But those who have had them not can never understand:
There is nothing so excruciating as sighs—
The sighs that refuse to be disposed of.
But they are removed by Amida,
And all I can say now is *Namu Amida Butsu, Namu Amida Butsu*!

Without the power of your truly mysterious working,
I would have long ago sunk into the depths of darkness and despair!

How do you see your own heart?
To see the heart, take Amida's mirror.
The wretchedness of my heart is like space, it has no limits.

To rejoice means to look forward to what lies in store:
Our impending birth in the Pure Land.
It means to be joyful while still here in this *Saha** world.

Nothing is left to Saichi,
Except a joyful heart, nothing is left to him.
Neither good nor bad has he, all is taken away from him;
Nothing is left to him!

---

* *Saha* is Sanskrit for 'endurance' and is often used to refer to our world where hardships must be borne.

VOICES OF LIGHT

To have nothing—how completely satisfying!
Everything has been carried away by the *Namu Amida Butsu*.

Your compassion is a sweet compassion,
A sweet joy that you laid upon me.

The sea is just full of water;
There is the seabed that sustains it.
Saichi is just full of evil karma;
There is Amida that sustains it.
How happy I am!

The adorable form of *Nyorai*
Is indeed this wretched self's form
Namu Amida Butsu, Namu Amida Butsu!

Saichi, you are so miserable.
Miserable I am but I see the sparkles,
I see the sparkles.*

My deluded thoughts are still there, no doubt about it.
And this is something our *Oya* allows,
For they become the seeds of our joy in Dharma.
Until life's end, they will go hand in hand with me.
How this makes me feel happy all over.

Saichi, how will you spend your future?
I'll spend it in the mercy of Amida.

Where have Saichi's desires gone?
They are still here:
I hate, I love, I crave. . . .

Parent's mind and child's mind,
Between them there is no restraint.
Namu Amida Butsu is both Parent's 'Come' and Child's 'Yes.'

---

* "We are all lying in the gutter, but some of us are looking at the stars."
(Oscar Wilde, 1854–1900)

ZUIKEN S. INAGAKI (1885–1981)

The Death Barrier, what does it mean to you?

Though my lodging has already been arranged,
    I am freezing in the snow as dusk gathers around me.

Birth-and-death is a matter of great importance;
    And Impermanence is quickly approaching.
Are you prepared?

Namu Amida Butsu is the *Tathāgata*'s life;
    It has found its way to me and become my life.
Mother and child share the same life;
    They breathe the same breath.

Morning and evening, the living Buddha, *Namu Amida Butsu*,
    comes in from my ears and goes out from my mouth.

This world is a dream indeed;
    Let us return to the home of Light.

No clouds hang in the sky of my mind any longer;
    I go to the Land of Bliss
        as Amida mindfully watches over me.

By day and by night, at all times,
    Amida's call of unfailing salvation
        touches the chord of my heart.

The *Tathāgata*'s living voice
    assuring me, 'Don't worry',
        Is *Namu Amida Butsu*.

Do you want peace of mind?
    If so, let peace of mind save you.
However, peace of mind does not take you to the Pure Land.
    By the Power of the Vow do you attain birth there.

Night is dark, and the road is not seen.
    At that moment, Amida offers his hand to guide me.
How great the Vow-Power is!

VOICES OF LIGHT

The course of the boat is left to the sail,
    the movement of the sail is left to the wind;
As for me, I leave everything to Amida.

The way a person of *shinjin* walks on the Great Path—
    without anxiety and without feigned peace of mind.

If you utter words from your deluded mind,
    all you say is false.

Let the Buddha-Dharma talk;
    Keep your mouth shut!

Without reverence and worship,
    you will not understand the Dharma.

Look up with a mind of no attachment;
    Stars sparkle in the sky.

Do not scold children;
    instead, show them what to do.
Let them imitate good Buddhists,
    If you really love them.

Do not speak ill of others; do not be proud.
    Humbling yourself, hold to the *nembutsu*.

Be careful about enjoyable things;
    If addicted to them, you will have cause for regrets.

For man's floating mind,
    there is no place to lodge, no port to stay.

When driven to the most difficult situation,
    You come face to face with your naked self and the *Tathāgata*.

Don't worry, don't worry!
    The mother of Great Compassion is waiting for you.

In daily life, selfish desires arise and anger fills my mind;
    Besides, I do not feel gratitude to Amida;
Yet Amida saves me just as I am;
    How grateful!

When I am alone oppressed by indescribable sadness,
    I feel that the compassion of my True Parent is trustworthy.

My calculations have proven futile;
    I follow my Parent's Call and return home.

I don't want to die, I don't want to die, I don't want to die;
    However reluctant to die, I cannot help but die.
        Nobody can help me—helplessly, I go to the Pure Land.

Death is coming closer and closer day by day;
     the law of karma is fearful indeed.
At the moment of realising this,
    we hear Amida's Call!
Boundless is your wisdom, like the open sky;
    Limitless is your compassion, like the great ocean.
I am at peace
    while my karma and spiritual hindrances remain intact.

Whilst living in this distasteful world,
    We can experience the joy of mindful recollection of the Buddha.
To what can this be compared?

If you have fully received the *Tathāgata*'s Compassion
    you naturally become kind to other people;
The secret of success is kindness.

Blown on, and by, the great wind of the Primal Vow,
    I surrender myself—wholly and effortlessly—to Amida.

Without being asked, he moves first,
    By calling 'Come, just as you are!'

In life or death, with the Buddha, the journey continues.

VOICES OF LIGHT

Hozen Seki (1903–1991)

The empty great sky always exists regardless of clouds, rain or the arising of any form. This empty sky embraces all forms. In the same way, Amida's compassion and wisdom are immeasurable ... and always shining.

So long as we have form, we cannot enter *Nirvāṇa* for form is the result of karma. When our form comes to an end, then we will enter *Nirvāṇa* through the Vow of Amida Buddha. That is the teaching of the Pure Land school.

We human beings are also Amida Buddha's transformed body and mind. That is the oneness of all life. Our inmost self is the infinite Life and Light of Amida Buddha. Unfortunately, we cannot understand this thoroughly, so we must suffer.

There are no borders to Amida's land; it is *everywhere.*

The relationship of the individual to *Nirvāṇa* is like that of waves to the water itself. There are many kinds of waves, some long, some short, some large, some small; but the waves cannot exist without the water. And when the 'karma' of wind stops blowing, the waves return completely to the water.

Death itself is not suffering—only the thinking of death makes for suffering. Death is the birth of *higan*, the Other Shore, the formless Absolute, the natural law of eternal time and infinite space.

Amida vows to save all beings without exception. But when we doubt his Vow, our mind is then floating this way and that; therefore, there is no true happiness. There are many such people, for doubting is a very common inclination. But even those floating will one day be born ... in the Pure Land.

There is a proverb: 'Those who enter the mountain, cannot see the mountain.' This is because the mountain is so large. Amida Buddha's compassion is too vast to be seen. But we are fortunate: even though we cannot see Amida's light, we are assuredly in it.

The teaching of the *nembutsu* is simple and profound. The Buddha-

Dharma—the law of the universe that has no colour, no form, no taste, and which is invisible and untouchable—manifests itself as Amida Buddha to save all sentient beings as they are. When we understand Amida's compassion in our heart, we appreciate this and are satisfied to be born in his Pure Land. Naturally, we call his name with gratitude.

Our ultimate purpose for living must be to seek that happiness which is beyond the world of birth-and-death. That happiness is the unconditioned compassion of Amida; and when we meditate on it, we feel truly happy. This is the only happiness that can rise above change, impermanence, self and suffering.

Today I believe in the Buddha . . . tomorrow I may not. What is of value is the infinite compassion and unconditional embrace of Amida, regardless of whether I believe or not.

We love; but this love is limited, impure and cannot last forever. Our love for others is always for our ego satisfaction. So, in this world, we try to extend our sympathy or care to others but it is always an imperfect, interrupted love. However, we do wish to work for the welfare of mankind. Everyone has sympathy for others in his innermost heart; but it is impossible to fully realise in this world.

Had I no passions, there would be no connection with Amida. Therefore, our passions are themselves the condition of Amida's embrace.

In *Nirvāṇa*, there is no desire, no karma—only absolute freedom that is infinite.

The mind of Amida Buddha is the Great Compassion. . . . When we are sunk in the deepest worldly ocean, Amida is also with us. He never asks for our prayers, our confessions, our faith or our cries to be saved.

Our existence is like a bubble on the surface of the water. Some day, some time, the bubble shall return to the water itself. We, the bubbles, cannot go anywhere but to the land of Amida Buddha. This is natural and unconditional, and the way of all sentient beings.

Until we leave this world, we cannot rely upon or hold anything—

health, body, material goods—except the *nembutsu*, the oneness of all life, in which limited self and unlimited Amida Buddha come together. *Nembutsu* is the returning home.

Amida Buddha is calling us day and night, 'Come to me as you are. Your existence is temporary, your life in this world is limited. Your limited life and my infinite life are one. You will return into my life through the *nembutsu*.'

If there were no people, no cats, no flowers—there would be no Amida; only the *Dharmakāya* would be said to 'exist.'

Nirvāṇa is like a spinning top that seems to be still, not moving, at rest. Yet it is poised on its tip, spinning very fast—so fast that you cannot see that it is in action; yet its appearance is of stillness. So stillness and activity seem here alike—but they are very different.

Amida's light is beyond form and matter.

The Way of *Nembutsu* is the way of true freedom, peace and permanence. In this world, we cannot obtain true freedom—there are always obstructions. Our life is temporary, not permanent, and we do not have true peace.

Every being will be born in the Pure Land. However, if one will not hear this teaching, one repeats birth-and-death, or suffering, until one finally hears.

In the Shin teaching, the main thing is to recite the *nembutsu* out of gratitude for the compassion of Amida Buddha. Then we will naturally refrain from evil and try to do good. So, concerning the doing of good, Other-Power is an easier way, the way of appreciation.

In Japan, we say: 'Let us taste Amida's teaching' instead of 'Let us believe Amida's teaching.' ... A lump of sugar is understandable through science; but that is only knowledge, not experience. Its sweetness is only known by experience. We are living in Amida Buddha's light and life, which it is very important to taste. Once we so taste, our thinking will be changed, even though we live in darkness and ignorance now.

There are many things to take refuge in, or be attached to, such as houses, philosophies, religions, material goods—and all of these are temporary. The last resort is the Infinite itself—Amida.

A dinner invitation for a delicious meal includes the condition: *Formal Dress*. But a poor person cannot buy or rent a tuxedo. Thus, even wanting to go, he is not suited for the invitation; and the invitation is not suited to him. 'Come As You Are' reads another invitation. This invitation is suitable for all. There are many teachings but this—that of Amida Buddha—is an invitation open to everyone.

At the end of his life, Shinran still confessed to how pitiful and shameful his mind was. A hypocritical person cannot express his own inward self. To show one's inwardness requires great courage.

I do not think that my faith is true, permanent or valuable. My faith is also my own illusion; therefore my faith has no value. As Rennyo said: 'The meaning of faith is *Truth-Mind*; this is not the mind of man . . . it is Amida's mind, not ours.' Faith or belief is always changing. I think this is true of me. . . . My practice is only to hear the call. Then I give thanks.

The moment of faith is Amida calling himself.

In this world there is first lightning, then thunder. The two really happen together, but the thunder is perceived later than the lightning. Even if we fail to see the light, still, the sound of the thunder assures us that it is flashing. To hear is to know of the light. To hear the *nembutsu* is to know the light of Amida's immeasurable wisdom and compassion; it is truly to *hear the Light*.

Amida Buddha is always watching, protecting and living in our dark hearts.

Our love is limited and does not last long—there is always a *condition*. When the condition is destroyed, then our love is destroyed with it. Compassion is beyond love. Compassion goes forth, *without conditions*, to others. We human beings cannot have compassion; what we have is love. Compassion belongs to Amida Buddha.

As Gautama Buddha said: 'Even if I try to express Amida Buddha and his land with my words, I would not be able to explain this wonderful bliss for all eternity. So accept this inexpressible Buddha, Amida.'

If we were enlightened in this world, our mind would be pure calm, clear—no wind of anger, greed, desire, ambition. But actually we cannot live in such a state of mind.

Regardless of our mind or actions—whether they be good or bad— Amida's boat is crossing the ocean of birth-and-death. Therefore it is of no value, and unnecessary, to grasp with my hand in doubt or to relax with an open hand. Belief or doubt are nonsense in the boat of Amida.

Everyone must be able to reach Buddhahood and, at this very moment, we are granted a promise of it.

If I visit Mr Jones and wish to drink his liquor and he only gives me a few drops, begrudgingly, I keep asking for more. However, when I visit Mr Smith, the liquor-maker, I am surrounded by liquors and can drink all I want—but I *won't*, out of concern for my health. This is the morality of freedom in true *shinjin*.

Higan—the 'Other Shore', *Nirvāṇa*, the Pure Land. *This* shore, or world, is a place full of disagreeable affairs, stealing, war, anger, hunger, desire. But the *other* shore is *Nirvāṇa*, beyond karma; it is true peace, freedom and happiness so, naturally, we look for the Other Shore.

Death is not destruction or annihilation or disappearance. Rather it is *freedom* that we experience at death—perfect, total freedom . . . and it is liberation from all suffering.

According to our teaching, a person's karma is absorbed by the greater 'karma' of Amida Buddha.

Queen Vaidehi asked Gautama Buddha for a way for suffering beings to see the Pure Land. The Buddha said that one ought to face the sunset and to concentrate or meditate on it, seeing it as a large red drum, sinking. Then, with eyes opened or closed, one will still see it. . . . Many people suffer from worldly desires . . . and cannot change their minds. But the Buddha says to look at the sunset and forget everything. Then our mind expands and connects to the Great Universe. . . .

When we truly understand our innermost self, we will understand and trust the teaching of Amida Buddha. This teaching is natural; for example, water has various forms according to temperature: steam, ice, snow, mist. But every form has the water nature. Even humans, plants and animals—all living things can be said to have the water nature, without which they cannot exist. One Mind is like this water nature. With Amida Buddha we are unified in One Mind. Shinran says that our existence is like ice—cold, hard; but, at the end of life, our ice will melt into the One Mind of Amida Buddha. To understand and accept this 'water nature'—Buddha Nature—is our salvation.

Many think that happiness is to pile up material goods—money, houses, clothing, trips. But this happiness is not continuous—misery is always waiting. Someone says that health is happiness—but this happiness is not continuous. Or someone thinks that living in this world is happiness—but we must die one day. Fame and knowledge, too, are happiness and misery mixed.

It is impossible to enter *Nirvāṇa* in this body, in this life. *Nirvāṇa* is only possible through Amida's unconditional embrace.

We have form. Buddha has no form. . . . Those who have form understand clearly only *other* forms. . . . Amida's vows are transcendental, truly beyond our comprehension. To aid our grasp and appreciation of their splendour, Shakyamuni Buddha uses language rich in colours, scents and textures.

From my side, when I say the *nembutsu*, it is the echo of Amida's calling; it is not my virtue or practice.

Amida Buddha's business is to save us; so we cannot interfere. But there are many who think that, unless a person rejoices in salvation, they will not be born in the Pure Land; or that the *nembutsu* must be recited earnestly; or that it is necessary to remember the moment of the arising of *shinjin*; or that the condition of one's mind must be such-and-such: all interfere with Amida's business.

Zen speaks of the 'sound of one hand clapping' and this involves difficulty for the student; one will say that he has heard the sound, another will lament that he has not. But in Shin it is easier—we hear the sound of two hands clapping: Amida and I in oneness, the sound being the *nembutsu*.

The time of hearing Amida's teaching is the best and most beneficial time of our entire lives.... It is not an accidental happening but is rather due to many past aeons of good karma.

Nembutsu is an expression of gratitude, not a deed of merit.... The feeling of gratitude is the strongest way of happiness for living in this world. If the *nembutsu* is virtue or good practice to me, I will worry when I cannot recite it or feel proud when I do.

In the Buddha's realm, all is beautiful down to the smallest jot. Everything will have this peaceful beauty *each in its own way*. Everyone will have their own value, beautiful to the smallest part—whereas in this world we discriminate and remain in less than complete beauty.

Sometimes when we hear of Amida Buddha's embrace, at first we feel very grateful and joyful. But this feeling will disappear [and so] has no value. Regardless of our gratitude or not, Amida is still calling. This is the natural compassion of the Universe. Therefore, we do not count on our feelings since these are based, after all, on passions. Passion *is* our mind.

Shinjin—when we consider this our own, we are in error; it is Amida's *shinjin*, Amida's faith in me. My 'faith' is of no value.... *Shinjin* and *nembutsu* are not from one's own side but from Amida Buddha. From this comes assurance and the mere recitation of the *nembutsu* in *shinjin* is the proof.

When we meditate on the true nature of the universe and every sentient being, we will realise, as Gautama Buddha said, that all life is oneness. So we do not and cannot live alone. And when we pass away from this world, we enter into infinite Life and Light. This is not 'my own' life and light—it belongs to all sentient beings.

Death is the birth of eternal blessing, the entrance to the Pure Land and a very happy occasion. However, we do not recognise this happiness because we are human beings... and worldly desire is very strong.

The air we are breathing here is the same air breathed in Africa, Asia, Europe. All sentient beings are living in the same condition. This is the teaching of Gautama Buddha. And every sentient being will be enlightened—not just humans, but cats and dogs, birds and fish—and all are my brothers and sisters. More than a thousand years ago, the Bodhisattva Gyōgi sang of walking through the forest:

> I heard the singing birds;
> Suddenly I thought:
> This is father's voice, mother's voice.

Biographical Index

ASAṄGA (300–370)
Indian scholar who is considered, along with his half-brother Vasubandhu, as the founder of the *Yogācāra* school of Buddhism. His principal work is the *Summary of the Great Vehicle*.

BANDŌ, Shōjun (1932–2004)
Japanese scholar and priest who was influential in disseminating Shin Buddhism in the West.

BYLES, Marie (1900–1979)
Australian explorer, conservationist, pacifist and solicitor who was also a travel and non-fiction writer. She embraced Pure Land Buddhism towards the end of her life.

CHANG PO-TUAN (983–1082)
Chinese Taoist mystic of the Sung Dynasty.

CH'EN TZU-ANG (656–698)
Chinese poet of the T'ang Dynasty.

CONZE, Edward (1904–1979)
Anglo-German scholar known for his pioneering translations of the *Prajñāpāramitā* or *Perfection of Wisdom* sutras.

DEVALA [n.d.]
Indian *brahmin*, also known as Asita, who was famous for supernatural powers developed through his mastery of meditation. It was he who divined that the future Buddha, Gautama, had been born as the son of King Suddhodana, ruler of the Shakya people.

DŌGEN (1200–1253)
Japanese monk regarded as the founder of the *Sōtō* school of Zen Buddhism.

DOLPOPA (1292–1361)
Tibetan Buddhist scholar who was as an early master of the *Jo Nang* lineage.

EMPEROR GO-TOBA (1180–1239)
The 82nd emperor of Japan.

EMPRESS KŌKEN (718–770)
The 46th and 48th monarch of Japan (also known as Empress Shōtoku during her second period of reign).

FUJII, Ryuchi (1892–1986)
Shin Buddhist priest who served as minister-in-charge of the Hilo temple in Hawaii. Author of *The True Meaning of Buddhism*, published in 1957.

GAMPOPA (1079–1153)
Founder of the *Kagyü* order of Tibetan Buddhism and the foremost student of Milarepa.

GENSHIN (942–1017)
Japanese monk of the *Tendai* school who was an influential advocate of Pure Land beliefs and practice. Renowned in his time for the highly influential treatise, *Ōjōyōshū*, he is regarded as the sixth patriarch of Shin Buddhism.

GISHIN (781–833)
A Japanese monk who became the first head of the *Tendai* school on Mount Hiei.

GYŌGI (670–749)
Japanese monk of the *Hossō* school and a major figure in the Buddhism of the Nara period, who attained great renown as a popular teacher and practicioner of good works.

HAGURI, Gyodo (1881–1965)
A Shin Buddhist priest who served congregations in both Japan and the United States. Author of *The Awareness of Self* which was published posthumously in 1967.

HAKEDA, Yoshito (1924–1983)
Japanese scholar and priest of the *Shingon* school, he was Professor of Religion at Columbia University in New York.

HAKUIN (1686–1768)
Japanese master famous for revitalising the *Rinzai* school of Zen Buddhism.

HATANI, Ryōtai (1883–1974)
Japanese scholar who taught at Ryukoku University in Kyoto and also served as a director of the Society for the Promotion of Buddhism.

BIOGRAPHICAL INDEX

Hōnen (1133–1212)
A major figure in Japanese Buddhism who founded the first independent Pure Land school, known as *Jōdo-shū*. He is considered the seventh patriarch of Shin Buddhism.

Huang Po (d. 850)
An influential master of Zen Buddhism during the T'ang Dynasty.

Hui-neng (638–713)
Chinese monk renowned for his great influence on *Ch'an* Buddhism (Zen), of which is he is regarded as the sixth, and final, patriarch.

Hui-Shih (380–305 BCE)
A philosopher who was an eminent representative of the early Chinese school of thought known as *The Dialecticians* during the 'Warring States' period (475–221 BCE).

Hui-Yüan (334–416)
Chinese monk who played a crucial role in the early development of Pure Land doctrines, especially through his establishment of the White Lotus Society.

Inagaki, Zuiken S. (1885–1981)
Shin Buddhist thinker who embraced a universalist view of the *Mahāyāna* teachings, drawing insights and inspiration from all its schools. He was a master in the *Horai* ('Dharma Thunder') lineage of the Shin tradition.

Ippen (1234–1289)
Japanese itinerant preacher who founded the *Ji-shū* school of Pure Land Buddhism.

Jōgan (1168–1251)
Originally a priest of the *Shingon* school, he was a student of esoteric Buddhism before finally becoming a disciple of Hōnen, after which he retired to a hermitage.

Jōkei (1155–1213)
A prominent Japanese Buddhist priest of the *Hossō* school.

Jōkō [n.d.]
A Pure Land priest of obscure provenance.

KAKUBAN (1095–1143)
Japanese monk and founder of the 'Shingi' branch of the *Shingon* school, who explored the esoteric aspects of Pure Land practice.

KAKUNYO (1270–1351)
The third *Monshu* ('Head-Priest') of the Japanese *Hongwanji* school of Shin Buddhism. He was the first to compile an account of the life of Shinran, who was his great-grandfather.

KAMO NO CHŌMEI (1155–1216)
Japanese author and poet who later became a Buddhist hermit. Famous for his work, *The Ten-Foot Square Hut.*

KANEKO, Daiei (1881–1976)
Japanese priest and leading Shin Buddhist thinker of the modern period. He was a Professor at Otani University in Kyoto.

KENKŌ (1283–1352)
Japanese writer and Buddhist monk, renowned for his *Essays in Idleness.*

KENSHŌ [n.d.]
Itinerant monk of the medieval period who practiced on Mount Kōya in Japan.

KING AŚOKA (304–232 BCE)
Indian emperor of the Maurya Dynasty and celebrated patron of Buddhism.

KINTAYU, Hori (1688–1755)
A master Japanese Zen swordsman.

K'UEI-CHI (632–682)
Scholar-monk of the T'ang Dynasty and founder of the *Faxiang Zong* school of Chinese Buddhism.

KŪKAI (774–835)
Founder of the *Shingon* school of Japanese Buddhism as well as an accomplished calligrapher, poet, engineer and sculptor. He is said to have invented *kana*, the Japanese syllabary. The Emperor Daigo granted him the posthumous title of *Kōbō-Daishi* ('Great Master Who Spread the Dharma') in 921.

KYEONG-HEUNG (*fl.* 7th century)
Korean master of Pure Land Buddhism.

BIOGRAPHICAL INDEX

KYŌBUTSU (*fl.* 13th century)
An itinerant Buddhist monk who lived on Mount Kōya in Japan.

KYŌRENJA (1199–1281)
A teacher of the Pure Land school who was active in spreading its doctrines throughout the Kamakura region of Japan.

MANSEI (*fl.* 8th century)
Japanese Buddhist priest and poet.

MILAREPA (1052–1135)
Famous Tibetan *yogi* and poet, as well as a major figure in the history of the *Kagyü* order.

MOTOKIYO, Zeami (1373–1455)
Japanese actor and playwright. His treatises on *Noh* theatre are the oldest known works on the philosophy of drama in Japanese literature.

MYŌHEN (1142–1224)
Reclusive priest and leading figure in the formation of the *hijiri*, or itinerant monks, of Mount Kōya.

MYŌZEN (1167–1242)
Japanese scholar-monk of the Tendai school who attained the high clerical rank of 'Dharma Seal'. He later converted to the Pure Land teachings following an encounter with Hōnen.

NĀGĀRJUNA (C. 150–250)
Indian Buddhist philosopher traditionally regarded as founder of the *Mādhyamika* school. He is also considered the first patriarch of Shin Buddhism.

O-KARU (1801–1856)
A poor laywoman who worked as a farmer on the Japanese island of Mutsure. She is considered a *myōkōnin* ('truly wondrous person' of faith) in the Shin Buddhist tradition.

PADAMPA SANGYE (d. 1117)
Indian tantric master renowned in Tibet.

PADMASAMBHAVA (*fl.* 8th century)
Legendary Indian Buddhist master widely revered in Tibet.

PALLIS, Marco (1895–1989)
Anglo-Greek writer and widely respected author on the Tibetan tradition who, towards the end of his life, became increasingly drawn to Shin Buddhism.

PRINCE SHŌTOKU (574–622)
Statesman of the Asuka Period who played an important role in the early dissemination of Buddhism in Japan.

RENNYO (1415–1499)
The eighth *Monshu* ('Head-Priest') of the Japanese *Hongwanji* school of Shin Buddhism. He played a vital role in consolidating the fortunes of this tradition for which he was celebrated as the 'Second Founder'.

RHYS DAVIDS, Caroline (1857–1942)
Prominent scholar of Pāli Buddhism who taught in the School of Oriental Studies at the University of London.

RYŌKAN (1758–1831)
Japanese poet and monk of the *Sōtō* school of Zen Buddhism.

SAICHI, Asahara (1850–1932)
A devout *myōkōnin* of Shin Buddhism, he was a poor tradesman who made clogs. He would jot down his verses on wooden shavings and his poems are estimated to have numbered upwards of ten thousand.

SARAHA (*fl.* circa 8th century)
Indian tantric adept who composed many spiritual songs and is regarded as one of the founders of the *Mahāmudrā* tradition of Buddhist esotericism.

SEIKAKU (1166–1235)
Japanese Tendai priest famous for the eloquence of his sermons. He later became a prominent disciple of Hōnen, founder of the *Jōdo* school of Pure Land Buddhism.

SEKI, Hozen (1903–1991)
Shin Buddhist priest who moved to the United States from Japan in order to undertake missionary work. He founded the New York Buddhist Church in 1937 and the American Buddhist Academy in 1948. His principal work was *The Great Natural Way* published in 1976.

BIOGRAPHICAL INDEX

SHAKU HANNYA (*fl.* 1920s)
A Buddhist scholar active in the early part of the 20th century and an authority on the *Heart Sūtra*.

SHAN-TAO (613–681)
A widely influential master of the Pure Land tradition in China and considered the fifth patriarch of Shin Buddhism. He was famous for his *Parable of the White Path*.

SHANTIDEVA (*fl.* 8th century)
Indian monk and scholar of the *Mādhyamika* school, particularly famous for his long poem on the practice of the bodhisattva path, the *Bodhicaryāvatāra*.

SHICHIRI, Gōjun (1835–1900)
A popular priest and very influential propagator of Shin Buddhism. A prolific writer, he was given the highest recognition of academic attainment (*kangaku*) shortly following his death.

SHINRAN (1173–1263)
Pupil of Hōnen and founder of the *Jōdo Shinshū*; also known as Shin, it is the largest school of Buddhism in Japan.

SHŌKŌ (1162–1238)
Japanese Tendai monk who studied under Hōnen in later life.

SHŌKŪ (1177–1247)
Disciple of Hōnen and an adherent of the Seizan branch of the *Jōdo* school of Pure Land Buddhism.

SOSHUN (1262–1336)
Chinese monk who moved to Japan and became spiritual adviser to the Emperor Go-Daigo before being made abbot of a Zen monastery in Kamakura.

STEWART, Harold (1916–1995)
Australian Shin Buddhist poet and thinker who spent the last thirty years of his life in Japan. His principal work, *By the Old Walls of Kyoto*, was published in 1981.

SUZUKI, Beatrice Lane (1878–1939)
American Buddhist scholar who was an effective populariser of *Mahāyāna* Buddhism in the West. She undertook graduate studies

at Columbia University and later married D.T. Suzuki with whom she collaborated on many projects.

SUZUKI, Daisetz Teitaro (1870–1966)
Renowned Japanese Zen scholar who also wrote extensively on *Mahāyāna* thought, generally, as well as on Shin Buddhism.

TAKUAN (1573–1645)
Japanese Zen master in the *Rinzai* tradition who was also adept in swordsmanship and gardening.

T'AN-LUAN (476–572)
Chinese monk who effected a successful synthesis of the *Mādhyamika* and *Yogācāra* schools in his interpretation of the Pure Land teachings. He is considered the third patriarch of Shin Buddhism.

TAO-CH'O (562–645)
A Chinese Buddhist scholar of the *Nirvāṇa Sūtra* who subsequently embraced the Pure Land tradition. He is considered the fourth patriarch of Shin Buddhism.

TATSUGUCHI, Wasui (b. 1930)
Shin Buddhist minister from Honolulu, Hawaii. Ordained in 1956, he completed his graduate studies at Ryukoku University in Kyoto and published *A Study of Shin Buddhism* in 1961.

TENSHITSU, Tōyo (*fl.* 16th century)
Japanese Zen master.

TSUNG-MI (780–841)
Chinese scholar-monk of the T'ang dynasty. He was the fifth and final patriarch of the *Hua-yen* school as well as a master of the *Ho-tse* lineage in the Southern tradition of *Ch'an* Buddhism.

T'U LUNG (1542–1605)
Chinese playwright and essayist from the Ming Dynasty.

UEDA, Yoshifumi (1904–1993)
Born into a Shin temple family, he was a distinguished scholar of *Mahāyāna* thought and a specialist in the *Yogācāra* school in particular. He founded the Department of Indian and Buddhist Philosophy at Nagoya University in Japan.

BIOGRAPHICAL INDEX

VASUBANDHU (*fl.* 4th century)
Indian monk who was exceptional in having made major contributions to all the main schools of Buddhist thought. He is said to have converted to the *Mahāyāna* tradition under the influence of his brother, Asanga. He is considered the second patriarch of Shin Buddhism and the 21st patriarch of Zen.

WANG AN-SHIH (1021–1086)
Chinese statesman, chancellor and poet of the Song Dynasty.

WONHYO (617–686)
Korean monk of the Silla Dynasty, renowned as both a great scholar and highly effective propagator of Buddhism among the laity.

YAMABE, Shūgaku (1882–1944)
Japanese Shin Buddhist scholar of the early 20th century.

YAMANOUE NO OKURA (660–733)
Japanese poet known for his poems about children and ordinary people.

YŌKAN (1032–1111)
Japanese precept master of the *Sanron* school who wrote several important works on Pure Land practice.

YUAN-CHAO (1048–1116)
Japanese Tendai priest who advocated a doctrine combining Pure Land thought with the observation of *vinaya* discipline and precepts.

ZENSHŌ (1174–1258)
Japanese Tendai monk who was a devotee of the Pure Land teachings and became an important disciple of Hōnen.

ZONKAKU (1290–1373)
Shin Buddhist scholar; son of Kakunyo (the third Head-Priest of the school) who was denied succession to this hereditary position by his own father as a result of an estranged relationship. He maintained broad relations with all the major Buddhist schools of his time and was a creative thinker who also enjoyed widespread popularity among followers.

Sources

The quotations in this work are drawn from the following sources and have, where appropriate, been slightly adapted for clarity and consistency. They have also been rendered into British English in keeping with the style observed in the rest of this work.

ABE Masao, *Zen and Western Thought* (Honolulu: University of Hawaii Press, 1985).

BANDO Shojun, 'Shinran's Indebtedness to T'an-luan', *Studies in Comparative Religion* (Vol. 5, No. 4, Autumn 1971).

BANDO Shojun, 'Significance of the Nembutsu', *Studies in Comparative Religion* (Vol. 6, No. 4, Autumn 1972).

BLOCKER H. Gene & STARLING Christopher L., *Japanese Philosophy* (Albany: SUNY Press, 2001).

BLOFELD John (tr.), *The Zen Teaching of Hui Hai* (London: Rider & Co., 1974).

BLOOM Alfred (ed.), *The Shin Buddhist Classical Tradition: A Reader in Pure Land Teaching* (Volume 1) (Bloomington: World Wisdom, 2013).

BLOOM Alfred (ed.), *The Shin Buddhist Classical Tradition: A Reader in Pure Land Teaching* (Volume 2) (Bloomington: World Wisdom, 2014).

BODHI Bhikkhu (tr.), *In the Buddha's Words: An Anthology of Discourses from the Pali Canon* (Boston: Wisdom Publications, 2005).

BROWN Brian Edward, *The Buddha Nature—A Study of the Tathāgatagarbha and Ālayavijñāna* (Motilal Banarsidass: Delhi 1991).

CLEARY Thomas (tr.), *The Flower Ornament Scripture* (Boston: Shambala, 1993).

SOURCES

CONZE Edward, *Buddhism: Its Essence and Development* (New York: Harper & Row, 1975).

COATES Havelock Harper & ISHIKUZA Ryugaku (tr.), *Honen the Buddhist Saint: His Life and Teachings* (Tokyo: Kodokaku, 1930).

CROUCHER Paul, *Buddhism in Australia* (Sydney: University of New South Wales Press, 1989).

DHAMMIKA Ven. S. (tr.), *The Edicts of King Ashoka* (Kandy: Buddhist Publication Society, 1993).

EVANS-WENTZ W.Y. (ed.), *Tibet's Great Yogi Milarepa* (Oxford: Oxford University Press, 1951).

FITZGERALD Joseph A. (ed.), *Honen the Buddhist Saint: Essential Writings and Official Biography* (Bloomington: World Wisdom, 2006).

FUJII Ryuchi, *The True Meaning of Buddhism* (Kyoto: Honpa Hongwanji Press, 1957).

GREGORY Peter N. (tr), *Inquiry Into the Origin of Humanity: An Annotated Translation of Tsung-mi's* Yüan jen lun *with a Modern Commentary* (Honolulu: University of Hawai'i Press, 1995).

HAGURI Gyodo, *The Awareness of Self: A Guide to the Understanding of Shin Buddhism* (Kyoto, 1967).

HAKEDA Yoshito (tr.), *The Awakening of Faith* (New York: Columbia University Press, 1967).

HAKEDA Yoshito (tr.), *Kūkai: Major Works* (New York: Columbia University Press, 1972).

HATANI Ryotai, *Realisation of Buddhist Nirvana* (Kyoto: Department of West Hongwanji, 1926).

HIROTA Dennis (tr.), *Plain Words on the Pure Land Way: Sayings of the Wandering Monks of Medieval Japan* (Kyoto: Ryukoku University, 1989).

HIROTA Dennis (tr.), *No Abode: The Record of Ippen* (Honolulu: University of Hawaii Press, 1998).

HONEN, *Words of Dharma* (San Francisco: Arya Marga Foundation, 1994).

HOPKINS Jeffrey (tr.), *Mountain Doctrine: Tibet's Fundamental Treatise on Other-Emptiness and the Buddha Matrix* (New York: Snow Lion Publications, 2006).

INAGAKI Hisao (tr.), *Anjin: Zuiken's Sayings* (Kyoto: Nagata Bunshodo, 1988).

INAGAKI Hisao (tr.), *Zuiken's Shinshu Dharma-Pada* (Kyoto: Nagata Bunshodo, 2006).

INAGAKI Hisao (tr.), *Goichidaiki-kikigaki 'Thus I Have Heard From Rennyo Shonin'* (Craiova: Dharma Lion Publications, 2008).

INAGAKI Hisao, *Shingon Philosophy and the Nembutsu* (Singapore: Horai Association, 2011).

ISHIDA Hoyu (tr.), *Myōkōnin O-Karu and Her Poems of Shinjin* (Kyoto: Nagata Bunshodo, 1991).

JEONG Byeong-Jo, *Master Wonhyo: An Overview of His Life and Teachings* (Seoul: Diamond Sutra Recitation Group, 2010).

KAZANTZAKIS Nikos, *A Journal of Two Voyages to the Far East* (Berkeley: Creative Arts Book Company, 1982).

KEENAN John P. (tr.), *Summary of the Great Vehicle* (Berkeley: Numata Center, 1992).

KEENE Donald (ed.), *Anthology of Japanese Literature* (London: Penguin, 1968).

KEENE Donald (tr.), *Essays in Idleness* (New York: Columbia University Press, 1998).

KIYOTA Minoru, *Shingon Buddhism: Theory and Practice* (Los Angeles & Tokyo: Buddhist Books International, 1978).

KUBO Tsugunari & YUYAMA Akira (tr.), *The Lotus Sūtra* (Berkeley: Numata Center, 1993).

LUK Charles (tr.), *The Śūraṅgama Sūtra* (London: Rider & Company, 1966).

SOURCES

MASCARÓ Juan (tr.), *The Dhammapada* (London: Penguin, 1973).

MATSUNAGA Daigan & Alicia, *Foundation of Japanese Buddhism* (Los Angeles & Tokyo: Buddhist Books International, 1974).

MCKINNEY Meredith (tr.), *Essays in Idleness* and *Hōjōki* (London: Penguin, 2014).

PALLIS Marco, *A Buddhist Spectrum* (London: George Allen & Unwin, 1980).

PAUL Diana Y. (tr.), *The Sutra of Queen Śrīmālā of the Lion's Roar* (Berkeley: Numata Center, 2004).

PERRY Whitall N. (ed.), *A Treasury of Traditional Wisdom* (Cambridge: Quinta Essentia, 1991).

PYE Michael (ed.), *Listening to Shin Buddhism* (Sheffield: Equinox, 2012).

PYE Michael (ed.), *Lay Buddhism and Spirituality* (Sheffield: Equinox, 2014).

RENNYO, *Letters* (Kyoto: Hongwanji International Center, 2000).

SEKI, Hozen, *The Great Natural Way* (New York: American Buddhist Academy, 1976).

SHANTIDEVA, *Bodhisattvacharyāvatāra* (Dharamsala: Library of Tibetan Works and Archives, 1979).

SHIH Heng-ching (tr.), *A Comprehensive Commentary on the Heart Sūtra* (Berkeley: Numata Center, 2001).

SHINRAN, *Collected Works* (Kyoto: Jodo Shinshu Hongwanji-ha, 1997).

STEARNS Cyrus, *The Buddha from Dolpo* (Albany: State University of New York Press, 1999).

STEVENS John, *Dewdrops on a Lotus Leaf: Zen Poems of Ryōkan* (Boston: Shambala, 1993).

STEWART Harold, *By the Old Walls of Kyoto: A Year's Cycle of Landscape Poems with Prose Commentaries* (New York: Weatherhill, 1981).

STODDART William, *The Essentials of Buddhist Spirituality* (Bloomington: World Wisdom, 2013).

SUZUKI Beatrice Lane, *Mahayana Buddhism* (London: Allen & Unwin, 1981).

SUZUKI Daisetz T., *A Miscellany on the Shin Teaching of Buddhism* (Kyoto: Shinshu Otaniha Shumusho, 1949).

SUZUKI Daisetz T., *Mysticism: Christian and Buddhist* (London: George Allen & Unwin, 1957).

SUZUKI Daisetz T., *Outlines of Mahayana Buddhism* (Schocken: New York, 1963).

SUZUKI Daisetz T., *Zen and Japanese Culture* (London: Taylor & Francis, 1970).

SUZUKI Daisetz T., 'The Buddhist Concept of Reality', *The Eastern Buddhist*, Vol. VII, No. 2 (October 1974).

SWANSON Paul (tr.), *The Collected Teachings of the Tendai Lotus School* (Berkeley: Numata Center, 1995).

TANAKA Eizo (tr.), '*Anjin-ketsujo-sho*: The Attainment of True Faith', *The Pure Land* (Nos. 2/2–5/2, December 1980–December 1983).

TATSUGUCHI Wasui, *A Study of Shin Budhism* (Honolulu: Shinshu Kyokai Mission of Hawaii, 1961).

UEDA Yoshifumi (ed.), *Letters of Shinran* (Kyoto: Hongwanji International Center, 1978).

VAN BRAGT Jan, 'Some Comparative Reflections On the Diverging Uses of Desire in Buddhism, Christianity and Jodo Shinshu', *The Pure Land* (New Series Nos. 10–11, December 1994).

WATSON Burton (tr.), *The Lotus Sutra* (New York: Columbia University Press, 1993).

WATSON Burton (tr.), *Four Huts: Asian Writings on the Simple Life* (Boston: Shambala, 2002).

WONHYO, *Selected Works* (Seoul: Jogye Order, 2012).

The author is a Shin Buddhist priest from Australia. His previous work, *Call of the Infinite*, has also been published in French, Italian and Greek editions.

www.ingramcontent.com/pod-product-compliance
Lightning Source LLC
Chambersburg PA
CBHW032101080426
42733CB00006B/363